Test Prep Series

GRE®
Wordlist:
491 Essential Words

491 Must Know words for the GRE®

Synonyms, antonyms & parts of speech

Context-based correct usage of words through sample sentences

Simplified pronunciation system to get familiar with the words easily

GRE® Wordlist: 491 Essential Words

© 2018, By Vibrant Publishers, USA. All rights reserved. No part of this publication may be reproduced or distributed in any form or by any means, or stored in a database or retrieval system, without the prior permission of the publisher.

ISBN-10: 1-946383-40-6
ISBN-13: 978-1-946383-40-2
Library of Congress Control Number: 2012916198

This publication is designed to provide accurate and authoritative information in regard to the subject matter covered. The Author has made every effort in the preparation of this book to ensure the accuracy of the information. However, information in this book is sold without warranty either expressed or implied. The Author or the Publisher will not be liable for any damages caused or alleged to be caused either directly or indirectly by this book.

Vibrant Publishers books are available at special quantity discount for sales promotions, or for use in corporate training programs. For more information please write to **bulkorders@vibrantpublishers.com**

Please email feedback / corrections (technical, grammatical or spelling) to **spellerrors@vibrantpublishers.com**

To access the complete catalogue of Vibrant Publishers, visit **www.vibrantpublishers.com**

GRE is the registered trademark of the Educational Testing Service (ETS) which neither sponsors nor endorses this product.

Table of Contents

Chapter 1	Abate - Attenuate	7
Chapter 2	Audacious - Controvert	19
Chapter 3	Conundrum - Dormant	31
Chapter 4	Downcast - Flag	43
Chapter 5	Flamboyant - Incoherent	55
Chapter 6	Incongruity - Metamorphosis	67
Chapter 7	Meticulous - Piety	79
Chapter 8	Pious - Redolent	91
Chapter 9	Refractory - Supersede	103
Chapter 10	Supposition - Yeoman	115

Preface

In the current format adopted by the GRE, verbal reasoning skills are given greater importance than ever. Students will face new types of questions in reading comprehension, sentence equivalence and text completion, and the average difficulty-level has gone up. The greater focus now is to test how well the student understands the context and is able to infer the right conclusions. This means merely learning vocabulary words by rote is not a good idea. Students looking to crack the verbal reasoning section need to develop a broader understanding of the vocabulary and relevant context.

This book was developed precisely with that purpose in mind. It presents **491 words for the GRE** that are most likely to appear in the test in different ways. The emphasis is on complete understanding rather than just word-meanings. Synonyms, antonyms and parts of speech are included to expand your thinking horizons. A simplified pronunciation system will help you get comfortable with how the words sound, and will be useful even long after you've cracked the GRE. Another great feature is the use of sample sentences that demonstrate the correct context for using the words. All this helps students improve cognitive and inferential thinking skills.

We suggest you have fun with these words. Don't just read them from the book, but make use of them in your daily conversations. Before long you'll start noticing them everywhere around you – in books, magazines, newspapers and movies. Use of **FLASH CARDS** is highly recommended to make these words permanent in your memory and breeze through the GRE.

Here's to your success!

Dear Student,

Thank you for purchasing **GRE® Wordlist: 491 Essential Words**. We are committed to publishing books that are content-rich, concise and approachable enabling more students to read and make the fullest use of them. We hope this book provides the most enriching learning experience as you prepare for your **GRE** exam.

Should you have any questions or suggestions, feel free to email us at reachus@vibrantpublishers.com

Thanks again for your purchase. Good luck for your GRE!

- Vibrant Publishers Team

facebook.com/vibrantpublishers

50% OFF

on MockTestPrep's – 10 Tests Pack for the GRE® Exam

Coupon: 10TESTS
www.mocktestprep.com

Valid through 01/31/2019

Other GRE Books in Test Prep Series

Verbal Insights on the GRE General Test
ISBN: 978-1-946383-36-5

Analytical Writing Insights on the GRE General Test
ISBN: 978-1-946383-39-6

GRE Analytical Writing: Solutions to the Real Essay Topics - Book 1
ISBN: 978-1-946383-26-6

GRE Analytical Writing: Solutions to the Real Essay Topics - Book 2
ISBN: 978-1-946383-29-7

Math Insights on the GRE General Test
ISBN: 978-1-946383-38-9

GRE Text Completion and Sentence Equivalence Practice Questions
ISBN: 978-1-946383-32-7

GRE Reading Comprehension: Detailed Solutions to 325 Questions
ISBN: 978-1-946383-30-3

GRE Master Word List: 1535 Words for Verbal Mastery
ISBN: 978-1-946383-41-9

GRE Word List: 491 Essential Words
ISBN: 978-1-946383-40-2

6 Practice Tests for the GRE
ISBN: 978-1-946383-34-1

GRE Words in Context: List 1
ISBN: 978-1-946383-42-6

GRE Words in Context: List 2
ISBN: 978-1-946383-43-3

GRE Words in Context: Challenging List
ISBN: 978-1-946383-44-0

Conquer the GRE: Stress Management & A Perfect Study Plan
ISBN: 978-1-946383-45-7

For the most updated list of books visit
www.vibrantpublishers.com

facebook.com/vibrantpublishers

Chapter 1

(Abate - Attenuate)

This chapter covers the following words along with their part of speech, pronunciation, synonyms and antonym, if applicable. Sample usage of the word is also illustrated.

abate
aberrant
abeyance
aboriginal
abscond
abstemious
acuity
admonish
adulterate
adverse
adversity
aesthetic
aggregate
alacrity
alias
alleviate
amalgamate
ambiguous
ambivalence
ameliorate

amend
amulet
anachronism
analogous
analogy
anarchy
anomalous
antecedents
anthology
antipathy
antiseptic
apathy
appease
apprise
approbation
appropriate
appurtenances
arboretum
archives
arduous

arrogance
artless
ascetic
assay
assiduous
assimilate
assuage
astigmatism
atrocity
attenuate

ABATE (v) *[uh-BEYT]*

Syn: reduce; subside; decrease; lessen; slacken; wane; moderate

Ant: increase; extend; amplify; continue; enlarge

Usage: By the next morning, the flood waters had *abated* considerably.

ABERRANT (adj) *[uh-BER-uh nt]*

Syn: abnormal; deviant

Ant: normal

Usage: Recently Jim's behavior has been noted to be *aberrant*.

ABEYANCE (n) *[uh-BEY-uh ns]*

Syn: suspended action; inactivity; cessation; suspension

Ant: continuance

Usage: But these rights of adulthood are in *abeyance* during the period of pupilage or nonage.

ABORIGINAL (adj) *[ab-uh-rij-uh-nl]*

Syn: being the first of its kind in a region; native

Ant: non-native

Usage: Members of the *aboriginal* tribes now live mainly in the central mountains.

ABSCOND (v) *[ab-SKOND]*

Syn: depart secretly and hide

Ant: appear; emerge; show; stay; remain

Usage: The culprit is said to be *absconding* with the bank robbery proceeds.

Chapter 1

ABSTEMIOUS (adj) *[ab-STEE-mee-uh s]*

Syn: Sparing in eating and drinking; temperate

Ant: intemperate; gluttonous; greedy

Usage: Roderick chooses to remain *abstemious* when the rest of his colleagues meet up for drinks.

ACUITY (n) *[uh-KYOO-i-tee]*

Syn: sharpness

Ant: stupidity

Usage: His sense of *acuity* and acumen was amazingly sharp even at this age.

ADMONISH (v) *[ad-MON-ish]*

Syn: warn; reprove

Ant: acclaim; commend; praise; compliment

Usage: His mother severely *admonished* him for running across the road in the midst of the chaotic traffic.

ADULTERATE (v) *[uh-DUHL-tuh-reyt]*

Syn: to make impure by adding inferior or tainted substances

Ant: purify; refine; improve

Usage: These days, even a simple food product like sugar is *adulterated* with pieces of contamination, so the FDA has brought in new regulations for manufacturers' compliance.

ADVERSE (adj) *[ad-VURS]*

Syn: unfavorable; hostile

Ant: favorable; propitious; fortunate; amicable; lucky

Usage: If you commit a crime, be prepared to suffer the *adverse* consequences.

ADVERSITY (n) *[ad-VUR-si-tee]*

Syn: poverty; misfortune

Ant: good luck; fortune; prosperity

Usage: They say the true strength of man is measured in times of *adversity*.

AESTHETIC (adj) *[es-THET-ik]*

Syn: artistic; dealing with or capable of appreciation of the beautiful

Ant: displeasing; unattractive

Usage: The new house does not have much *aesthetic* appeal.

AGGREGATE (v) *[AG-ri-geyt]*

Syn: sum; accumulate; amount to

Ant: separate; dissipate; disperse; divide; segregate

Usage: The mangoes stolen from the farm will *aggregate* to five or six dozen.

ALACRITY (n) *[uh-LAK-ri-tee]*

Syn: cheerful promptness; eagerness; celerity; willingness; cheerfulness

Ant: aversion; slowness; repugnance; reluctance; unwillingness

Usage: On hearing the good news, the three of them rose to their feet with such *alacrity* that he was stunned.

ALIAS (n) *[EY-lee-uh s]*

Syn: an assumed name

Ant: given name

Usage: His most commonly used *alias* was "Jack Smith."

ALLEVIATE (v) *[uh-LEE-vee-eyt]*

Syn: relieve

(Abate – Attenuate)

Ant: exacerbate; aggravate; increase; augment; embitter

Usage: With great patience, he set out to *alleviate* their uneasiness.

AMALGAMATE (v) *[uh-MAL-guh-meyt]*

Syn: blend; combine; unite in one body

Ant: separate; decompose; disintegrate; disunite

Usage: The two small companies decided to *amalgamate* to form a bigger one.

AMBIGUOUS (adj) *[am-BIG-yoo-uh s]*

Syn: unclear or doubtful in meaning; obscure; uncertain

Ant: indisputable; obvious; unequivocal; unambiguous

Usage: It would be far more sensible to write clear, lucid statements than *ambiguous* statements, which would only serve to confuse the reader.

AMBIVALENCE (n) *[am-BIV-uh-luh ns]*

Syn: the state of having contradictory or conflicting emotional attitudes

Ant: certainty; decisiveness

Usage: Paul was faced with deep *ambivalence* toward the prevailing culture.

AMELIORATE (v) *[uh-MEEL-yuh-reyt]*

Syn: improve

Ant: injure; spoil; mar; debase; deteriorate

Usage: The weather *ameliorated* toward the evening, with a beautiful sunset and pleasant temperatures.

AMEND (v) *[uh-MEND]*

Syn: correct; change; generally for the better

Ant: impair; injure

Usage: After twenty years of bitter quarrel, the son now wanted to *amend* his relationship with his father so they could spend some time together before it was too late.

AMULET (n) *[AM-yuh-lit]*

Syn: charm; talisman

Usage: Father William then tied a black *amulet* around Harry's arm and said that it was a good luck charm to protect him from evil.

ANACHRONISM (n) *[uh-NAK-ruh-niz-uh m]*

Syn: something or someone misplaced in time

Usage: The appearance of a printed book in a movie about Plato was a major *anachronism* because the printing press was not invented until 1700 years after his death.

ANALOGOUS (adj) *[uh-NAL-uh-guh s]*

Syn: comparable

Ant: dissimilar; unlike

Usage: Sitting in the seat of that game port is *analogous* to sitting in a plane; the game completely simulates the feeling of flying in an airplane.

ANALOGY (n) *[uh-NAL-uh-jee]*

Syn: similarity; parallelism

Ant: dissimilarity; disproportion; inequality; incongruity

Usage: To explain the concept of writing a program in a simpler manner, Bob used an *analogy* of cooking a dish and listed out each step.

ANARCHY (n) *[AN-er-kee]*

Syn: absence of governing body; state of lawlessness and disorder

Ant: rule; order; lawfulness

Usage: There were riots, fights, and *anarchy* everywhere in the state.

ANOMALOUS (adj) [uh-NOM-uh-luh s]

Syn: abnormal; irregular

Ant: usual; normal; regular

Usage: His behavior was getting to be abnormal and *anomalous.*

ANTECEDENTS (n) [an-tuh-SEED-nts]

Syn: preceding events or circumstances that influence what comes later; ancestors or early background

Ant: descendents

Usage: The law firm wanted to perform a thorough check of his *antecedents.*

ANTHOLOGY (n) [an-thol-uh-jee]

Syn: book of literary selections by various authors

Usage: Last year the trust published an *anthology* of new dialect writing, called Still Life.

ANTIPATHY (n) [an-TIP-uh-thee]

Syn: extreme aversion; dislike; distaste; enmity

Ant: affinity; amity; sympathy; attraction; harmony

Usage: The two warring brothers have a great amount of *antipathy* toward each other.

ANTISEPTIC (n) [an-tuh-SEP-tik]

Syn: substance that prevents infection

Usage: Savlon is one of the world's most popular *antiseptics.*

APATHY (n) *[AP-uh-thee]*

Syn: lack of caring; indifference; impassiveness

Ant: passion; sensibility; care; curiosity; zeal

Usage: With time, the people in larger cities are beginning to have more *apathy* towards civil issues.

APPEASE (v) *[uh-PEEZ]*

Syn: pacify or soothe; relieve

Ant: embitter; annoy; irritate; perturb; roil

Usage: Some primitive tribes believe that animals must be sacrificed in order to *appease* the gods.

APPRISE (v) *[uh-PRAHYZ]*

Syn: inform; tell; advise

Ant: keep secret

Usage: No matter what the consequence would be, we knew we had to *apprise* the boss about the loss of data.

APPROBATION (n) *[ap-ruh-BEY-shuh n]*

Syn: approval; praise

Ant: criticism; disapprobation; denial; censure; refusal

Usage: She desperately sought *approbation* for her actions from her peers.

APPROPRIATE (v) *[uh-PROH-pree-eyt]*

Syn: acquire; take possession of for one's own use

Ant: give away; bequeath; bestow

Usage: It is a crime to *appropriate* property that has been marked by someone else.

Chapter 1

APPURTENANCES (n) *[uh-PUR-tn-uh ns s]*

Syn: subordinate possessions; additions; accessories

Ant: requirements

Usage: We decided to buy at one go the whole set of *appurtenances* that would be needed for our new venture.

ARBORETUM (n) *[ahr-buh-REE-tuh m]*

Syn: botanic garden; place where different tree varieties are exhibited

Usage: Nina has an awesome *arboretum* with some rare eucalyptus, cypress, and pine trees.

ARCHIVES (n) *[AHR-kahyvs]*

Syn: public records; library; place where public records are kept

Usage: Newspaper *archives* are the best place to look for old, outdated articles.

ARDUOUS (adj) *[AHR-joo-uhs]*

Syn: hard; strenuous

Ant: easy; simple

Usage: It was a tiring, *arduous* climb to the clifftop.

ARROGANCE (n) *[AR-uh-guh ns]*

Syn: pride; haughtiness

Ant: humility; modesty; servility; bashfulness; diffidence; politeness

Usage: One of his most despicable qualities is his *arrogance*.

ARTLESS (adj) *[AHRT-lis]*

Syn: without guile; open and honest

Ant: secretive

Usage: Cathy seems such an *artless*, innocent young girl.

ASCETIC (adj) *[uh-SET-ik]*

Syn: practicing self-denial; austere

Ant: hedonistic; sociable

Usage: The *ascetic* life is just not Bob's cup of tea; he loves the material world too much.

ASSAY (v)/(n) *[a-SEY]*

Syn: analyze; evaluate

Usage: The professor said he would *assay* the documents in leisure and would let me know about their validity.

ASSIDUOUS (adj) *[uh-SIJ-oo-uh s]*

Syn: diligent; persevering

Ant: lazy; negligent

Usage: Sara is a committed, hardworking and *assiduous* worker.

ASSIMILATE (v) *[uh-SIM-uh-leyt]*

Syn: take in; absorb

Ant: dissimilate

Usage: Moose takes twice as much time as other guys to *assimilate* any bit of news we give him.

ASSUAGE (v) *[uh-SWEYZH]*

Syn: ease or lessen (pain); satisfy (hunger); soothe (anger)

Ant: estrange; excite; increase; provoke; inflame; incite; stimulate

Usage: The dentist talked to her gently and *assuaged* her fears before starting to work on her sore tooth.

ASTIGMATISM (n) *[uh-STIG-muh-tiz-uh m]*

Syn: eye defect that prevents proper focus

Ant: stigmatism

Usage: After giving me a series of eye tests, the ophthalmologist told me that I have *astigmatism*.

ATROCITY (n) *[uh-TROS-i-tee]*

Syn: brutal deed

Ant: good behavior

Usage: On the prison island of Alcataraz, numerous unspeakable *atrocities* are committed upon prisoners.

ATTENUATE (v) *[uh-TEN-yoo-eyt]*

Syn: make thin; weaken; contract

Ant: expand; increase; intensify; strengthen

Usage: The tight corset only seemed to *attenuate* her figure making her look thinner than ever.

This page is intentionally left blank

Chapter 2

(Audacious - Controvert)

This chapter covers the following words along with their part of speech, pronunciation, synonyms and antonym, if applicable. Sample usage of the word is also illustrated.

audacious
austere
austerity
autocrat
autonomous
autopsy
aver
banal
begrudge
belie
beneficent
berserk
billowing
blandishment
blowhard
boisterous
bolster
bombastic
burgeon
burnish

buxom
cacophonous
cadaverous
capricious
castigation
caustic
celerity
centrifugal
charlatan
chasten
chicanery
cipher
circlet
circuitous
coagulate
coda
cogent
commensurate
compendium
complaisant

compliant
concur
confound
connoisseur
consensus
consture
contention
contentious
contrite
controvert

AUDACIOUS (adj) *[aw-DEY-shuh s]*

Syn: daring; bold

Ant: cowardly; timid; feckless; diffident; introverted

Usage: Her *audacious* behavior shocked the entire crowd.

AUSTERE (adj) *[aw-STEER]*

Syn: forbiddingly stern; severely simple and unornamented

Ant: indulgent; genial; luxurious; mild; dissipated

Usage: A nun's simple and *austere* lifestyle was just not Gina's cup of tea; she was too used to material comforts.

AUSTERITY (n) *[aw-STER-i-tee]*

Syn: sternness; severity; refraining from luxuries

Ant: luxuriousness; indulgence

Usage: It is not an easy task to practice such *austerity* as the monks; it requires a strong will and determination in extremes.

AUTOCRAT (n) *[AW-tuh-krat]*

Syn: dictator

Ant: democrat

Usage: Pol Pot, the ruthless dictator of Cambodia, was an *autocrat* to the core.

AUTONOMOUS (adj) *[aw-TON-uh-muh s]*

Syn: self-governing; independent

Ant: dependent; subject

Usage: The company now functions as an *autonomous* unit without any supporting infrastructure.

AUTOPSY (n) *[AW-top-see]*

Syn: examination of a dead body; post-mortem

Usage: The police wanted permission from Dana's mother to perform an *autopsy* which they said would determine the cause and exact time of death.

AVER (v) *[uh-VUR]*

Syn: assert; state confidently

Ant: deny; protest

Usage: "Oh no, that's not true," she *averred*, when they suggested that she might be a manager.

BANAL (adj) *[buh-NAL]*

Syn: hackneyed; commonplace; trite; lacking originality

Ant: fresh; new; original

Usage: The conversation was too *banal* for her taste.

BEGRUDGE (v) *[bi-GRUHJ]*

Syn: resent; envy; covet

Ant: admit; concede

Usage: When I saw all the benefits Kylie received for her employee-of-the-month title I *begrudged* her the award.

BELIE (v) *[bi-LAHY]*

Syn: contradict; give a false impression

Ant: attest; prove

Usage: Wilma's modest, self-effacing attitude *belies* her intelligence and talents.

BENEFICENT (adj) *[buh-NEF-uh-suh nt]*

Syn: kindly; doing good; beneficial

Ant: cold-hearted; maleficent; malicious

Usage: Myra was interested to know if this event could be *beneficent* to her in any way.

BERSERK (adj) *[ber-SURK]*

Syn: frenzied

Ant: calm

Usage: The elephant went *berserk* on hearing the sudden sound of firecrackers and damaged a few stalls nearby before the mahout finally calmed the animal.

BILLOWING (adj) *[bil-oh-ing]*

Syn: swelling out in waves; surging

Ant: compact; shrinking

Usage: The *billowing* smoke from burning houses was a dreadful sight.

BLANDISHMENT (n) *[BLAN-dish-muh nt]*

Syn: flattery; exaggeration

Ant: disgust; repulsion

Usage: Fed up with the saleswoman's *blandishments*, we bought two of the items even though we didn't actually need them.

BLOWHARD (n) *[BLOH-hahrd]*

Syn: talkative boaster

Ant: milquetoast

Usage: Rod is just another *blowhard* who loves to brag about his supposedly great achievements; none of his peers take him seriously.

(Audacious – Controvert)

Chapter 2

BOISTEROUS (adj) *[BOI-ster-uh s]*

Syn: violent; rough; noisy

Ant: peaceful; calm; serene; self-possessed

Usage: The party was *boisterous* and loud, as usual.

BOLSTER (v) *[BOHL-ster]*

Syn: support; reinforce

Ant: hinder; obstruct; prevent

Usage: They *bolstered* their favorite participant's spirits by cheering for him at the top of their lungs.

BOMBASTIC (adj) *[bom-BAS-tik]*

Syn: pompous; using inflated language

Ant: humble

Usage: Making *bombastic* statements is easy enough; to prove that you really possess knowledge is quite tough.

BURGEON (v) *[BUR-juh n]*

Syn: grow forth; send out buds

Ant: atrophy

Usage: The venture seems to be *burgeoning* day by day.

BURNISH (v) *[BUR-nish]*

Syn: make shiny by rubbing; polish

Ant: dull

Usage: The table had been *burnished* with wax in preparation for his visit.

www.vibrantpublishers.com

BUXOM (adj) *[BUHK-suh m]*

Syn: plump; vigorous; jolly

Ant: flat; petite; small

Usage: A *buxom* young lady greeted us at the door.

CACOPHONOUS (adj) *[kuh-KOF-uh-nuh s]*

Syn: discordant; inharmonious

Ant: euphonious

Usage: I wonder how far she would get as a singer with that *cacophonous* voice.

CADAVEROUS (adj) *[kuh-DAV-er-uh s]*

Syn: like a corpse; pale

Ant: healthy; lifelike; flushed; lively

Usage: The prolonged illness had made her thin, pale, and *cadaverous*.

CAPRICIOUS (adj) *[kuh-PRISH-uh s]*

Syn: unpredictable; fickle; whimsical

Ant: steady; constant; dependable

Usage: Kenneth is too *capricious* to stay steady with the new job; he has been job-hopping continuously for the last two years.

CASTIGATION (n) *[KAS-ti-gey shun]*

Syn: punishment; severe criticism; chastisement; blame

Ant: exaltation; commendation; praise

Usage: Jenny knew she was in for a major *castigation* for having disobeyed the hostel warden's rules.

Chapter 2

CAUSTIC (adj) *[KAW-stik]*

Syn: burning; sarcastically biting

Ant: calm; mild; soothing

Usage: With her *caustic* remarks and sharp tongue, she is a terror among her peers.

CELERITY (n) *[suh-LER-i-tee]*

Syn: speed; rapidity

Ant: slowness; sluggishness; inertness; tardiness

Usage: We had to rush with *celerity*, for time was not on our side.

CENTRIFUGAL (adj) *[sen-TRIF-yuh-guh l]*

Syn: radiating; departing from the center

Ant: centripetal

Usage: The *centrifugal* force was powerful enough to rock us and make us tremble.

CHARLATAN (n) *[SHAHR-luh-tn]*

Syn: quack; pretender to knowledge

Ant: the real thing

Usage: The lady is a *charlatan*; no one trusts her to do legitimate business anymore.

CHASTEN (v) *[CHEY-suh n]*

Syn: discipline; punish in order to correct

Ant: encourage; uplift; benefit; assist

Usage: Her mother would *chasten* her all the time, thus ensuring that Sara grew up to be a decent young woman.

CHICANERY (n) [shi-KEY-nuh-ree]

Syn: trickery; deception

Ant: honesty

Usage: It's yet another of his tricks or *chicanery*; we refuse to believe him anymore.

CIPHER (n) [SAHY-fer]

Syn: secret code

Usage: The metal bracelet contained a secret *cipher* inside it.

CIRCLET (n) [SUR-klit]

Syn: small ring; band

Usage: The gold *circlet* on Anna's arm was badly damaged when she fell from the parapet, but she herself was barely injured.

CIRCUITOUS (adj) [ser-KYOO-i-tuh s]

Syn: roundabout

Ant: straight; direct; linear

Usage: I soon discovered that the cab driver was taking me along a *circuitous* route and demanded that he stop immediately.

COAGULATE (v) [koh-AG-yuh-lit]

Syn: thicken; congeal; clot

Ant: rarefy; expand; dissipate; thin; liquefy

Usage: The liquid gel was *coagulating* because of the cool temperature.

CODA (n) [KOH-duh]

Syn: concluding section of a musical or literary composition

(Audacious – Controvert)

Ant: introduction of a musical or literary composition

Usage: The *coda* is often more technically difficult to master than any other piece of music.

COGENT (adj) *[KOH-juh nt]*

Syn: convincing

Ant: weak; feeble; powerless; ineffectual

Usage: I was by now quite familiar with his *cogent,* persuasive tactics so I resisted being persuaded by them.

COMMENSURATE (adj) *[kuh-men-ser-it]*

Syn: equal in extent

Ant: lesser; greater

Usage: The letter said that the salary offered would be *commensurate* with the best in the industry.

COMPENDIUM (n) *[kuh m-PEN-dee-uh m]*

Syn: brief, comprehensive summary; abstract; abridgement

Ant: expansion; addition

Usage: The students were asked to submit a brief *compendium* of their annual project to the departmental head.

COMPLAISANT (adj) *[kuh m-pley-suh nt]*

Syn: trying to please; obliging; agreeable

Ant: antagonistic; disagreeable; obstinate

Usage: The man seemed to be over-obliging and *complaisant* to me.

COMPLIANT (adj) *[kuh m-PLAHY-uh nt]*

Syn: yielding

Ant: immutable

Usage: The students decided to be *compliant* with the school dress code to avoid having to serve detention for disobeying the rules.

CONCUR (v) *[kuh n-KUR]*

Syn: agree

Ant: differ; dissent; disagree; argue

Usage: We all *concurred* with the leader's decision.

CONFOUND (v) *[kon-FOUND]*

Syn: confuse; puzzle

Ant: elucidate; unravel; arrange; classify; enlighten

Usage: The more they tried to get details, the more the crime *confounded* them.

CONNOISSEUR (n) *[kon-uh-SUR]*

Syn: person competent to act as a judge of art, etc.; a lover of an art

Ant: ignoramus

Usage: Ken Smith is a *connoisseur* of arts and culture.

CONSENSUS (n) *[kuh n-SEN-suh s]*

Syn: general agreement

Ant: disagreement

Usage: The committee reached a *consensus* eventually, after hours of discussion on the issue, and passed the bill.

(Audacious – Controvert)

Chapter 2

CONSTRUE (v) *[kuh n-STROO]*

Syn: explain; interpret

Ant: scramble

Usage: What she had actually said and what was being *construed* by the manager were two different things.

CONTENTION (n) *[kuh n-TEN-shuh n]*

Syn: antagonism; strife

Ant: accord; agreement; harmony

Usage: It was a close *contention* with each faction getting as many votes as the other.

CONTENTIOUS (adj) *[kuh n-TEN-shuh s]*

Syn: quarrelsome

Ant: congenial; obliging; considerate; easy; passive

Usage: From a peaceful discussion it soon rose to a *contentious,* hot argument with both parties swearing at each other.

CONTRITE (adj) *[kuh n-TRAHYT]*

Syn: penitent

Ant: lacking remorse; unrepentant

Usage: Seeing her dismayed look on hearing my harsh words, I suddenly felt *contrite* and ashamed.

CONTROVERT (v) *[KON-truh-vurt]*

Syn: oppose with arguments; attempt to refute; contradict

Ant: agree; harmonize

Usage: They tried hard to make him confess but he *controverted* and opposed every statement they made and even brought in witnesses to support his logic.

Chapter 3

(Conundrum - Dormant)

This chapter covers the following words along with their part of speech, pronunciation, synonyms and antonym, if applicable. Sample usage of the word is also illustrated.

conundrum	dexterous	disseminate
converge	diatribe	dissolution
convoluted	dichotomy	dissonance
copious	didactic	distend
corollary	diffidence	distill
covert	diffuse	diverge
cozen	digression	divest
daunt	dirge	document
decorum	disabuse	dogmatic
default	discerning	dormant
deference	discordant	
delineate	discredit	
denigrate	discrete	
deride	disheveled	
derivative	disingenuous	
desecrate	disinterested	
desiccate	disjointed	
desultory	dismiss	
deterrent	disparate	
devout	dissemble	

CONUNDRUM (n) *[kuh-NUHN-druh m]*

Syn: riddle; puzzle; secret

Ant: common understanding

Usage: Paul was facing a unique *conundrum*, something of the kind he had never faced before in life and would require all of his wits to solve.

CONVERGE (v) *[kuh n-VURJ]*

Syn: approach; tend to meet; come together

Ant: diverge

Usage: She asked him to wait near the spot where the two roads *converged*.

CONVOLUTED (adj) *[KON-vuh-loo-tid]*

Syn: coiled around; involved; intricate

Ant: direct; straight

Usage: The route was too *convoluted* and complex for us to understand, so we hired a guide to lead us to the hills.

COPIOUS (adj) *[KOH-pee-uh s]*

Syn: plentiful

Ant: destitute; sparse

Usage: She was weeping *copiously* and all Jack could do was to look at her in helplessness; he was at a loss for words.

COROLLARY (n) *[KAWR-uh-ler-ee]*

Syn: conclusion; consequence

Usage: The *corollary* drawn by the defense lawyer on the basis of the evidence submitted was totally wrong, according to Peter.

COVERT (adj) *[KOH-vert]*

Syn: secret; hidden; clandestine

Ant: overt; exposed; open; revealed

Usage: The men had used *covert* tactics to get into the grounds at night and execute the crime by disarming the fence and killing the dogs silently.

COZEN (v) *[KUHZ-uh n]*

Syn: cheat; hoodwink; swindle; deceive

Ant: be honest

Usage: Polly is a very deceitful young woman; she has been known to *cozen* people out of their savings.

DAUNT (v) *[dawnt]*

Syn: intimidate; frighten

Ant: embolden; encourage; inspire

Usage: It was bad of the woodcutter to *daunt* and scare the little kids with his big axe.

DECORUM (n) *[di-KAWR-uh m]*

Syn: propriety; orderliness and good taste in manners

Ant: indecorum; impropriety; disturbance

Usage: The pupils were sternly instructed to observe *decorum* in the auditorium.

DEFAULT (n) *[di-FAWLT]*

Syn: failure to act; deficiency

Ant: advantage

Usage: He did not win the match through great performance but rather won it by *default* when his opponent failed to appear.

DEFERENCE (n) *[DEF-er-uh ns]*

Syn: courteous regard for another's wish

Ant: impoliteness; disobedience

Usage: In *deference* to the ladies present in the room, the men refrained from cracking lewd, bawdy jokes.

DELINEATE (v) *[di-LIN-ee-eyt]*

Syn: portray; depict; sketch

Ant: confuse; blur

Usage: He *delineated* his personal problems in great detail.

DENIGRATE (v) *[DEN-i-greyt]*

Syn: blacken; defame; slander

Ant: panegyrize; praise

Usage: Paul just loves to *denigrate* on Kim's faults in public, to her extreme annoyance.

DERIDE (v) *[di-RAHYD]*

Syn: ridicule; make fun of; scoff

Ant: applaud

Usage: Little Paul was scared that his peers in school would *deride* him for his misshapen outfit.

DERIVATIVE (adj) *[di-RIV-uh-tiv]*

Syn: unoriginal; derived from another source

Ant: original

Usage: The *derivative* outcome of the bill is the massive surge in employment.

(Conundrum – Dormant)

Chapter 3

DESECRATE (v) *[DES-i-kreyt]*

Syn: profane; violate the sanctity of

Ant: sanctify; consecrate; dedicate; employ; devote; purify; solemnize

Usage: Some vandals *desecrated* the revered leader's statue by garlanding it with a string of torn shoes.

DESICCATE (v) *[DES-i-keyt]*

Syn: dry up

Ant: moisten

Usage: The recipe required the use of dry and *desiccated* coconut.

DESULTORY (adj) *[DES-uh l-tawr-ee]*

Syn: aimless; haphazard; digressing at random

Ant: consecutive; serious; methodical; diligent; thorough; painstaking

Usage: Their *desultory* wandering for more than three hours in the woods ended in a collapse of fatigue near the stream.

DETERRENT (n) *[di-tur-uh nt]*

Syn: something that discourages or prevents; hindrance

Ant: catalyst; encouragement

Usage: Even that which we considered a major setback was not a *deterrent* for her, so determined and resolute was she in her pursuit of success.

DEVOUT (adj) *[di-VOUT]*

Syn: pious

Ant: atheistic; irreverent; ungodly; impious

Usage: He is a *devout* Christian and attends mass regularly, without fail.

DEXTEROUS (adj) *[DEK-struh s]*

Syn: adroit; skillful

Ant: clumsy; maladroit; awkward; unapt; inept

Usage: I had never come across anyone as *dexterous* and skillful as Harry.

DIATRIBE (n) *[DAHY-uh-trahyb]*

Syn: bitter scolding or harangue; invective; denunciation

Ant: praise; recommendation

Usage: Then there was an endless *diatribe* by his wife on why he should quit smoking.

DICHOTOMY (n) *[dahy-KOT-uh-mee]*

Syn: split; branching into two parts (especially contradictory ones)

Ant: unity

Usage: There is often a *dichotomy* between politicians' words and deeds.

DIDACTIC (adj) *[dahy-DAK-tik]*

Syn: teaching; instructional

Usage: Nick has always been academically inclined, so his *didactic* achievements were no surprise to his family.

DIFFIDENCE (n) *[DIF-i-duh ns]*

Syn: shyness; lack of confidence

Ant: audacity; arrogance; confidence

Usage: To alleviate the young boy's shyness and *diffidence,* George talked to him gently about books, music, and other subjects which might draw the boy's attention.

(Conundrum – Dormant)

Chapter 3

DIFFUSE (adj) *[di-FYOOS]*

Syn: wordy; rambling; spread out (like a gas)

Ant: terse; laconic; epigrammatic; condensed; concise

Usage: The report was unnecessarily *diffuse* and long-winded, instead of being short and succinct.

DIGRESSION (n) *[di-GRESH-uh n]*

Syn: wandering away from the subject

Ant: directness; straightness

Usage: The *digression* of the speaker every now and then from the subject of the lecture was getting tiresome.

DIRGE (n) *[durj]*

Syn: sad song; coronach

Usage: The ladies of the dead tribesman's family wailed loudly in a *dirge*.

DISABUSE (v) *[dis-uh-BYOOZ]*

Syn: correct a false impression; undeceive

Ant: deceive

Usage: He had a couple of detailed explanations ready with him to clarify and *disabuse* his position with the management.

DISCERNING (adj) *[di-SUR-ning]*

Syn: mentally quick and observant; having insight

Ant: obtuse

Usage: He is an extremely *discerning* supervisor; the slightest of faults in the products never escape his sharp gaze.

DISCORDANT (adj) *[dis-KAWR-dnt]*

Syn: not harmonious; conflicting

Ant: harmonious

Usage: In the midst of the lovely music suddenly some *discordant* tunes were heard, very jarring to the ears.

DISCREDIT (v) *[dis-KRED-it]*

Syn: defame; destroy confidence in; disbelieve

Ant: credit; honor; trust; believe; show faith

Usage: The seemingly harmless action had *discredited* his carefully earned goodwill among the villagers.

DISCRETE (adj) *[di-SKREET]*

Syn: separate; discontinuous; unconnected

Ant: attached; combined; joined

Usage: Discrete particles hold a great fascination for Mark and he has chosen to conduct an extensive research on them for his thesis.

DISHEVELED (adj) *[di-SHEV-uh ld]*

Syn: untidy

Ant: neat; orderly

Usage: A *disheveled,* shabby old man opened the door and asked us whom we wanted to see.

DISINGENUOUS (adj) *[dis-in-JEN-yoo-uh s]*

Syn: not naive; sophisticated; not straightforward

Ant: naive; ingenuous

Usage: His *disingenuous* and insincere means of achieving the monthly targets soon came to the notice of the manager and he was dismissed from the job.

(Conundrum – Dormant)

DISINTERESTED (adj) *[dis-IN-tuh-res-tid]*

Syn: unprejudiced; detached; uninvolved

Ant: biased; concerned; interested

Usage: He is *disinterested* in any form of sport or physical activity.

DISJOINTED (adj) *[dis-JOIN-tid]*

Syn: disconnected; loose

Ant: coherent; connected

Usage: He spoke in labored, *disjointed* phrases, so they all grew quiet straining to hear his every word.

DISMISS (v) *[dis-MIS]*

Syn: put away from consideration; reject

Ant: retain; detain; keep

Usage: He *dismissed* the reports of the bomb scare, saying that it was only a hoax and nothing to be afraid of.

DISPARATE (adj) *[DIS-per-it]*

Syn: unrelated; incomparable in quality; basically different

Ant: alike; equal; similar

Usage: They are as *disparate* as fire and ice.

DISSEMBLE (v) *[di-SEM-buh l]*

Syn: disguise; pretend

Ant: admit; allow

Usage: They accused the government of *dissembling* in their account of the use of funds.

DISSEMINATE (v) *[di-SEM-uh-neyt]*

Syn: distribute; spread; scatter (like seeds)

Ant: collect; gather

Usage: The news was then *disseminated* to all parts of the world through the various news channels.

DISSOLUTION (n) *[dis-uh-LOO-shuh n]*

Syn: disintegration; separation; looseness in morals

Ant: combination; connection; unification

Usage: The *dissolution* of the Parliament will take place at noon today.

DISSONANCE (n) *[DIS-uh-nuh ns]*

Syn: discord; disagreement

Ant: agreement; concord; harmony

Usage: The *dissonance* and din were making it difficult for us to hear each other.

DISTEND (v) *[di-STEND]*

Syn: expand; inflate; swell out

Ant: contract; reduce; shrink; narrow

Usage: His belly has become *distended* due to his gross eating habits.

DISTILL (v) *[di-STILL]*

Syn: extract the essence; purify; refine; concentrate

Ant: pollute

Usage: They *distilled* the liquid for months to make the new product.

Chapter 3

DIVERGE (v) *[di-VURJ]*

Syn: vary; go in different directions from the same point

Ant: converge

Usage: The river *diverged* into two streams near the base of the hill.

DIVEST (v) *[di-VEST]*

Syn: strip; deprive

Ant: invest

Usage: The highway hijackers then *divested* the female passengers of their ornaments and jewelry and made off with the loot.

DOCUMENT (v) *[dok-yuh-ment]*

Syn: provide written evidence

Ant: contradict; deny

Usage: The historians *documented* their findings in a series of reports.

DOGMATIC (adj) *[dawg-MAT-ik]*

Syn: opinionated; arbitrary; doctrinal

Ant: indecisive; flexible

Usage: Her *dogmatic* and rigid attitude often annoys the people around her.

DORMANT (adj) *[DAWR-muh nt]*

Syn: sleeping; lethargic; latent

Ant: operative; energetic; wakeful; vigilant

Usage: His childhood desire to fly a plane, *dormant* all these years, suddenly grew alive once more on seeing the aircraft at the hangar.

This page is intentionally left blank

Chapter 4

(Downcast - Flag)

This chapter covers the following words along with their part of speech, pronunciation, synonyms and antonym, if applicable. Sample usage of the word is also illustrated.

- downcast
- dupe
- dyspeptic
- eclectic
- efficacy
- effrontery
- effusion
- elegy
- elicit
- embellish
- embrace
- empirical
- emulate
- endearment
- endemic
- enervate
- engender
- enhance
- entail
- ephemeral
- epigram
- equanimity
- equipoise
- equivocate
- erode
- erroneous
- esoteric
- estranged
- eulogy
- euphemism
- exacerbate
- exasperate
- exceptionable
- exculpate
- exigency
- expansive
- expletive
- fabricate
- facetious
- facilitate
- fallacious
- fancied
- fastidious
- fatuous
- fawning
- felicitous
- fervor
- figurative
- flaccid
- flag

DOWNCAST (adj) *[DOUN-kast]*

Syn: disheartened; sad

Ant: upbeat

Usage: His face grew *downcast* and sad upon reading the Dear John letter.

DUPE (v) *[doop]*

Syn: fool; cheat

Ant: be honest

Usage: Beware of strangers who visit your house claiming to be long-lost acquaintances, for they could possibly *dupe* you and rob you.

DYSPEPTIC (adj) *[dis-PEP-tik]*

Syn: suffering from indigestion; crabby; grouchy

Ant: pleasant; cheerful

Usage: The landlady was upset at having taken in a *dyspeptic*, bad-tempered tenant, for she feared the other tenants might be disturbed by his presence.

ECLECTIC (adj) *[i-KLEK-tik]*

Syn: composed of elements selected from various sources

Ant: narrow; unvaried

Usage: I am glad to be part of such an *eclectic* group of people.

EFFICACY (n) *[EF-i-kuh-see]*

Syn: power to produce desired effect

Ant: inefficiency; uselessness; futility

Usage: The young woman's *efficacy* and diligence impressed me; I decided to give her a promotion at the year-end.

Chapter 4

EFFRONTERY (n) *[i-FRUHN-tuh-ree]*

Syn: shameless boldness

Ant: diffidence

Usage: The manager was taken aback to see the newly appointed salesman's *effrontery*; he certainly hadn't expected this kind of brash behavior from a newcomer.

EFFUSION (n) *[i-FYOO-zhuh n]*

Syn: outpouring; abundance

Ant: trickle

Usage: No one could resist the strong *effusion* of warmth which Mrs. Genet displayed.

ELEGY (n) *[EL-i-jee]*

Syn: poem or song expressing lamentation; dirge; epitaph

Ant: celebration

Usage: The poet decided to compose an *elegy* for his friend's funeral.

ELICIT (v) *[ih-LIS-it]*

Syn: evoke; draw out by discussion

Ant: draw in

Usage: No matter what I said, I failed to *elicit* any kind of response from the child.

EMBELLISH (v) *[em-BEL-ish]*

Syn: adorn; ornament

Ant: disfigure; deface; mar

Usage: Her gown was *embellished* with threaded designs of pure gold.

EMBRACE (v) *[em-breys]*

Syn: hug; adopt or espouse

Ant: release; let go

Usage: It was heartening to see a Labor government *embrace* most of the recommendations, including independence for the Bank of England.

EMPIRICAL (adj) *[em-PIR-i-kuh l]*

Syn: based on experience; practical

Ant: anecdotal; impractical; conjectural

Usage: The scientists based their conclusion on the *empirical* evidence from their many experiments.

EMULATE (v) *[EM-yuh-leyt]*

Syn: imitate; rival

Ant: abandon; leave

Usage: Kids love to *emulate* the behavior of their parents.

ENDEARMENT (n) *[en-DEER-muh nt]*

Syn: fond statement; attachment

Ant: animosity

Usage: He whispered sweet *endearments* into her ears and she giggled coyly.

ENDEMIC (adj) *[en-DEM-ik]*

Syn: prevailing among a specific group of people or in a specific area or a country

Ant: limited

Usage: The officials advised Karen to be quarantined in isolation because she had been diagnosed to have an *endemic* disease.

(Downcast – Flag)

ENERVATE (v) *[EN-er-veyt]*

Syn: weaken; tire

Ant: strengthen; energize

Usage: A sleepless night had *enervated* Jim and made him listless in the morning.

ENGENDER (v) *[en-JEN-der]*

Syn: cause; produce

Ant: stop; kill; finish

Usage: A small goof-up by a floor technician *engendered* a huge loss to the company.

ENHANCE (v) *[en-HANS]*

Syn: increase; improve

Ant: decrease; reduce; worsen

Usage: They have decided to *enhance* the features of the air-conditioning system so as to make it much more advanced and efficient.

ENTAIL (v) *[en-teyl]*

Syn: require; necessitate; involve

Ant: exclude; reject

Usage: We recognize that doing this may *entail* treating some pupils differently.

EPHEMERAL (adj) *[i-FEM-er-uh l]*

Syn: short-lived; fleeting

Ant: perpetual; endless; eternal; enduring; permanent

Usage: The pleasure was *ephemeral*, temporary, and not long-lasting or enduring.

EPIGRAM (n) *[EP-i-gram]*

Syn: witty thought or saying, usually short; aphorism

Usage: Everyone at the party looked forward to hearing Jason's witty jokes and epigrams.

EQUANIMITY (n) *[ee-kwuh-NIM-i-tee]*

Syn: calmness of temperament; composure; levelheadedness

Ant: agitation; anxiety

Usage: She did not lose her coolness and *equanimity* even in the face of such a terrible personal crisis.

EQUIPOISE (n) *[EE-kwuh-poiz]*

Syn: equilibrium; counterbalance; equality

Ant: difference; imbalance

Usage: Her carefully maintained *equipoise* collapsed upon hearing the shattering news; she broke down, crying copiously.

EQUIVOCATE (v) *[ih-KWIV-uh-keyt]*

Syn: avoid an issue; lie; mislead; attempt to conceal the truth

Ant: face; meet

Usage: I hadn't expected the Department of Justice to *equivocate* and evade the matter in this manner.

ERODE (v) *[ih-ROHD]*

Syn: eat away; deteriorate

Ant: build; construct

Usage: The powerful waves of the sea had *eroded* the rocks on the shore.

(Downcast – Flag)

ERRONEOUS (adj) *[uh-ROH-nee-uh s]*

Syn: mistaken; wrong

Ant: exact; correct

Usage: The editor of the newspaper was sued for printing *erroneous* facts about the minister.

ESOTERIC (adj) *[es-uh-TER-ik]*

Syn: hard to understand; known only to the chosen few

Ant: common; familiar; known

Usage: The trade agreement was framed in a rather *esoteric* manner according to Jake; it would be too difficult for a layman to understand it.

ESTRANGED (adj) *[ih-STREYNJD]*

Syn: separated; alienated

Ant: united

Usage: The couple has been *estranged* for almost a year now and will shortly divorce.

EULOGY (n) *[YOO-luh-jee]*

Syn: expression of praise, especially for someone who is dead

Ant: calumny; condemnation; criticism

Usage: On the spot, he decided to compose a *eulogy* in praise of the distinguished gentleman.

EUPHEMISM (n) *[YOO-fuh-miz-uh m]*

Syn: mild expression in place of an unpleasant one; circumlocution

Ant: bluntness

Usage: The prose was inundated with too many *euphemisms*, which was not to Neil's liking; he decided to edit the piece all over again.

EXACERBATE (v) *[ig-ZAS-er-beyt]*

Syn: worsen; embitter

Ant: alleviate; soothe

Usage: Watching the movie *exacerbated* his passion against the terrorists and he decided to enlist in the armed services as soon as possible.

EXASPERATE (v) *[ig-ZAS-puh-reyt]*

Syn: vex; upset; provoke

Ant: placate; mollify; calm; conciliate

Usage: I was *exasperated* by the slowness of the desk clerk in processing the application because he had already delayed it by three days.

EXCEPTIONABLE (adj) *[ik-sep-shuh-nuh-buhl]*

Syn: objectionable; disagreeable

Ant: pleasant; welcome

Usage: This action is normally taken only in *exceptionable* circumstances.

EXCULPATE (v) *[EK-skuhl-peyt]*

Syn: clear from blame

Ant: incriminate

Usage: It was thanks to the highly talented lawyer that Alan Burner had been *exculpated* of the charges and declared a free man.

EXIGENCY (n) *[EK-si-juh n-see]*

Syn: urgency; difficulty

Ant: tranquility

Usage: I wished they would display more *exigency* in winding up the construction because we were short of time and the new residents were to arrive any day.

(Downcast – Flag)

Chapter 4

EXPANSIVE (adj) *[ik-span-siv]*

Syn: broad; comprehensive; outgoing and sociable; extensive

Ant: limited; narrow

Usage: They played the kind of *expansive* rugby with which he most identified.

EXPLETIVE (n) *[EK-spli-tiv]*

Syn: interjection; profane oath; curse; exclamation

Ant: quiet; silence

Usage: I was offended by his use of an *expletive* in the sentence, and bluntly told him so.

FABRICATE (v) *[FAB-ri-keyt]*

Syn: manufacture; build; lie

Ant: demolish; spoil; break

Usage: The defense could not prove that the evidence was *fabricated* even though they kept insisting that was the case.

FACETIOUS (adj) *[fuh-SEE-shuh s]*

Syn: joking; humorous; sarcastic

Ant: grave; serious; dull; lugubrious

Usage: We all laughed at his *facetious* and hilarious attempt at poetry.

FACILITATE (v) *[fuh-SIL-i-teyt]*

Syn: help bring about; make less difficult

Ant: block; prohibit

Usage: The embassy did everything they could possibly do to *facilitate* the travel of the dignitaries to the remote island.

FALLACIOUS (adj) *[fuh-LEY-shuh s]*

Syn: false; misleading

Ant: truthful

Usage: The firm was shocked to discover that the employee had supplied a *fallacious* background and gained a foothold into its fold.

FANCIED (adj) *[FAN-seed]*

Syn: imagined; unreal

Ant: real; serious; unimaginative

Usage: It all seems part of her *fancied* ideas; however, nothing can be described concretely.

FASTIDIOUS (adj) *[fa-STID-ee-uh s]*

Syn: difficult to please; squeamish

Ant: lax; casual

Usage: Mrs. Williams is rather *fastidious*, so I was apprehensive about inviting her to my home; the kids were always making a mess and the house never looked clean and tidy.

FATUOUS (adj) *[FACH-oo-uh s]*

Syn: foolish; inane

Ant: intelligent; clever; sensible; knowledgeable

Usage: Freddie, being a *fatuous* and foolish boy, is always at the mercy of the other children who love to play silly pranks on him.

FAWNING (adj) *[fawn ing]*

Syn: courting favor by cringing and flattering; deferential; groveling

Ant: aloof; disinterested

Usage: I was irritated to see Mark flattering and *fawning* over Sara; she certainly didn't deserve the man's attentions.

FELICITOUS (adj) *[fi-LIS-i-tuh s]*

Syn: apt; suitably expressed; well-chosen

Ant: unfortunate

Usage: This seemed a *felicitous* and fitting occasion to inform Diana about her promotion.

FERVOR (n) *[FUR-ver]*

Syn: glowing ardor; intensity of feeling; excitement; enthusiasm

Ant: apathy; coolness

Usage: He immersed himself into the course with such *fervor* and enthusiasm that everyone who knew him was amazed.

FIGURATIVE (adj) *[FIG-yer-uh-tiv]*

Syn: not literal, but metaphorical; using a figure of speech

Ant: literal; straightforward

Usage: I could grasp the literal meaning of the prose but not its *figurative* significance.

FLACCID (adj) *[FLAS-sid]*

Syn: flabby

Ant: muscular

Usage: Her once-lustrous, bouncy hair now lay *flaccid* and dull upon her shoulders.

FLAG (v) *[flag]*

Syn: droop; grow feeble

Ant: revive; strengthen; restore

Usage: His interest in history class *flagged* when the pretty girl switched to a different session.

Chapter 5

(Flamboyant - Incoherent)

This chapter covers the following words along with their part of speech, pronunciation, synonyms and antonym, if applicable. Sample usage of the word is also illustrated.

flamboyant	goad	imperturbable
fledgling	gouge	impervious
flout	grandiloquent	implication
fluke	gregarious	implicit
flux	grueling	implode
foible	guileless	import
foment	gullible	imprudent
forebears	haggle	inadvertently
foreboding	harangue	inchoate
forestall	herbivorous	incoherent
franchise	hireling	
frugality	holster	
fulcrum	homogeneous	
futile	iconoclastic	
gainsay	idiosyncrasy	
garrulous	idolatry	
generality	immutable	
germane	impair	
gerrymander	impassive	
girth	impede	

FLAMBOYANT (adj) [flam-BOI-uh nt]

Syn: ornate; colorful; flashy

Ant: moderate; tasteful

Usage: Gerald's *flamboyant* taste in clothes has earned him many funny nicknames and sobriquets.

FLEDGLING (adj) [FLEJ-ling]

Syn: inexperienced

Ant: expert; professional

Usage: They are a group of *fledgling,* budding writers.

FLOUT (v) [flout]

Syn: reject; mock

Ant: honor; respect

Usage: He is always *flouting* the rules that are laid down and someday he is bound to face trouble.

FLUKE (n) [flook]

Syn: unlikely occurrence; stroke of fortune

Ant: certainty

Usage: She passed the exam just by *fluke.*

FLUX (n) [fluhks]

Syn: flow; series of changes

Ant: constancy; stability

Usage: The constant *flux* in his personal life caused his work performance to suffer.

(Flamboyant – Incoherent)

Chapter 5

FOIBLE (n) *[FOI-buh l]*

Syn: weakness; slight fault

Ant: strength

Usage: We were all aware of old Ben's *foibles* and peculiarities but he was such an adorable old man that no one minded him.

FOMENT (v) *[foh-MENT]*

Syn: stir up; instigate

Ant: dampen; dissuade

Usage: The movie *fomented* desires and passions that had been dormant within him.

FOREBEARS (n) *[FAWR-bairs]*

Syn: ancestors

Ant: descendents

Usage: The *forebears* of Thomas Wood provided a strong financial foundation for his current business success.

FOREBODING (n) *[fawr-BOH-ding]*

Syn: premonition of evil; misgiving; bad omen

Ant: fortune; providence

Usage: He had a strange sense of *foreboding* that things were about to go wrong.

FORESTALL (v) *[fohr-STAWL]*

Syn: prevent by taking action in advance

Ant: enable; promote

Usage: Before they could move on further, he *forestalled* them, saying they could not enter the haunted house.

FRANCHISE (n) *[FRAN-chahyz]*

Syn: right granted by authority; right to vote; business licensed to sell a product in a particular territory

Ant: obligation; disqualification; disability

Usage: The town population was rather reluctant to exercise their *franchise* to elect a leader of their choice.

FRUGALITY (n) *[FROO-guh l-i-tee]*

Syn: thrift; economy

Ant: generosity; wastefulness

Usage: Through years of *frugality* the woman saved enough money to buy herself the piano she had always dreamed of having.

FULCRUM (n) *[FOO L-kruh m]*

Syn: support on which a lever rests

Usage: The key to the power of the lever is the position of the *fulcrum* it rests upon.

FUTILE (adj) *[FYOOT-l]*

Syn: useless; hopeless; ineffectual

Ant: effective; powerful; cogent; useful; solid; capable

Usage: No matter how hard she worked, her efforts seemed *futile* because nothing much was getting accomplished.

GAINSAY (v) *[GEYN-sey]*

Syn: deny; contradict

Ant: affirm; verify; confirm; attest; witness

Usage: Her honesty meant no one could *gainsay* her conclusions.

(Flamboyant – Incoherent)

Chapter 5

GARRULOUS (adj) *[GAR-uh-luhs]*

Syn: loquacious; wordy; talkative

Ant: silent; speechless; taciturn; quiet

Usage: Nick is a *garrulous*, loquacious man who can barely resist an opening to start talking.

GENERALITY (n) *[jen-uh-RAL-i-tee]*

Syn: vague statement

Ant: specificity; detail

Usage: He avoided *generalities* and preferred to stick with facts.

GERMANE (adj) *[jer-MEYN]*

Syn: pertinent; bearing upon the case at hand; relevant

Ant: foreign; alien; irrelevant; unconnected

Usage: We wondered if the subject was *germane* to the situation.

GERRYMANDER (v) *[jer-i-man-der]*

Syn: change voting district lines in order to favor a political party

Usage: This redistricting looked like a clear attempt to *gerrymander* the boundaries to try to help the Conservatives.

GIRTH (n) *[gurth]*

Syn: distance around something; circumference

Usage: The man's *girth* had increased immensely since he had left the house and now his old trousers could no longer fit him.

GOAD (v) *[gohd]*

Syn: urge on

Ant: discourage

Usage: They *goaded* and egged him on to win the race.

GOUGE (v) *[gouj]*

Syn: tear out

Ant: fill in

Usage: The terrorists then *gouged* out his eyes and slashed his face many times before throwing him into the woods.

GRANDILOQUENT (adj) *[gran-DIL-uh-kwuh nt]*

Syn: pompous; bombastic; using high-sounding language

Ant: humble; unpretentious; plain; unadorned

Usage: The wedding celebrations were in his inimitable, *grandiloquent* style.

GREGARIOUS (adj) *[gri-GAIR-ee-uh s]*

Syn: sociable; extroverted

Ant: introverted

Usage: Karen is such a *gregarious* person; she loves to be surrounded by people.

GRUELING (adj) *[GROO-uh-ling]*

Syn: exhausting

Ant: refreshing; relaxing

Usage: The trip had been very tiring and *grueling* so Jim took an additional two days off to rest and relax.

GUILELESS (adj) *[GAHYL-lis]*

Syn: without deceit; honest

(Flamboyant – Incoherent)

Chapter 5

Ant: artful; cunning; deceitful

Usage: I was taken aback by the sheer honesty and *guileless* attitude of the young man.

GULLIBLE (adj) *[GUHL-uh-buh l]*

Syn: easily deceived

Ant: discerning

Usage: Ben is too *gullible*; anyone can easily cheat him and get away with it too.

HAGGLE (n) *[HAG-uh l]*

Syn: argue about prices; bicker; quarrel

Ant: agree; comply

Usage: We didn't have the patience to *haggle* with the shopkeeper for a lesser rate so we paid him the price he quoted and moved on.

HARANGUE (n) *[huh-RANG]*

Syn: noisy speech; long lecture

Ant: conversation

Usage: Kenneth Parker then launched into a long and tiresome *harangue* on why the public should vote for the Democrats.

HERBIVOROUS (adj) *[hur-BIV-er-uh s]*

Syn: plant-eating; vegetarian

Ant: carnivorous; meat-eating

Usage: Tom Jones has earned the sobriquet of *"herbivorous* creature" on account of his fondness for plants.

HIRELING (n) *[HAHYUHR-ling]*

Syn: one who serves for hire (usually used contemptuously)

Ant: boss

Usage: Jack didn't like the *hireling* of the mafia man talking to him in such an audacious manner.

HOLSTER (n) *[HOHL-ster]*

Syn: pistol case

Usage: I could see a gun peeking out from his shoulder *holster*.

HOMOGENEOUS (adj) *[hoh-muh-JEE-nee-uh s]*

Syn: of the same kind

Ant: heterogeneous

Usage: The *homogeneous* mixture in the bottle was blue in color and emitted a strange odor.

ICONOCLASTIC (adj) *[ahy-KON-uh-klast-ic]*

Syn: attacking cherished traditions; skeptical

Ant: traditionalist; orthodox

Usage: James Bean has always been *iconoclastic,* never conforming to the trend but always treading his own path.

IDIOSYNCRASY (n) *[id-ee-uh-SING-kruh-see]*

Syn: individual trait usually odd in nature; eccentricity

Ant: conformity

Usage: Old Zaya is full of *idiosyncrasies* of which even her grandchildren make fun.

Chapter 5

IDOLATRY (n) *[ahy-DOL-uh-tree]*

Syn: worship of idols; excessive admiration

Ant: disapproval; disrespect

Usage: The college dean frowned at the girl's acts of *idolatry* in the presence of the visiting rock star.

IMMUTABLE (adj) *[ih-myoo-tuh-buhl]*

Syn: unchangeable

Ant: changeable; flexible; variable

Usage: The point is that you can save yourself from many sorts of mistakes by making files *immutable*.

IMPAIR (v) *[im-PAIR]*

Syn: worsen; diminish in value

Ant: enhance; improve; augment; repair; increase; build up; perfect

Usage: The chemicals had *impaired* his vision to some extent.

IMPASSIVE (adj) *[im-PAS-iv]*

Syn: without feeling; imperturbable; stoical

Ant: passionate

Usage: Unperturbed, he shot an *impassive* look at her in response to her challenging statement.

IMPEDE (v) *[im-PEED]*

Syn: hinder; block

Ant: assist

Usage: Nothing could now *impede* his progress since he was so determined to achieve his goal.

IMPERTURBABLE (adj) [im-per-TUR-buh-buh l]

Syn: calm; placid; composed

Ant: anxious

Usage: His face looked *imperturbable*, not giving away his response to the accusation.

IMPERVIOUS (adj) [im-PUR-vee-uh s]

Syn: impenetrable; incapable of being damaged or distressed

Ant: penetrable; explorable; pregnable

Usage: He is seemingly *impervious* to any harm.

IMPLICATION (n) [im-pli-KEY-shuh n]

Syn: something hinted at or suggested

Ant: fact; blunt accusation

Usage: The *implications* of the President's statement were yet to be analyzed.

IMPLICIT (adj) [im-PLIS-it]

Syn: understood but not stated; implied

Ant: explicit

Usage: Her assent was *implicit*. Although she did not explicitly agree, it was assumed that she'd said yes.

IMPLODE (v) [im-PLOHD]

Syn: burst inward

Ant: explode

Usage: The bomb caused the mansion to *implode*.

(Flamboyant – Incoherent)

IMPORT (n) *[IM-pawrt]*

Syn: significance

Ant: insignificance

Usage: I thought deeply, trying to gather the *import* of his statements.

IMPRUDENT (adj) *[im-PROOD-nt]*

Syn: Lacking caution; injudicious

Ant: prudent

Usage: It was *imprudent* of her to ask the question at the ceremony.

INADVERTENTLY (adv) *[in-uh d-VUR-tnt ly]*

Syn: unintentionally; by oversight; carelessly

Ant: intentionally

Usage: He *inadvertently* called her by her name even though she had forbidden him to do so.

INCHOATE (adj) *[in-KOH-it]*

Syn: recently begun; rudimentary; elementary

Ant: long-lasting

Usage: The *inchoate* production of the play was enough to make us realize we would never wish to see the finished work.

INCOHERENT (adj) *[in-koh-HEER-uh nt]*

Syn: unintelligible; muddled; illogical

Ant: coherent; clear; continuous; intelligible

Usage: They were trying hard to decipher the dying man's *incoherent* ramblings.

Chapter 6

(Incongruity - Metamorphosis)

This chapter covers the following words along with their part of speech, pronunciation, synonyms and antonym, if applicable. Sample usage of the word is also illustrated.

incongruity	irascible	malign
inconsequential	irremediable	malingerer
incorporate	irresolute	malleable
indeterminate	itinerary	martinet
indigence	jettison	maverick
indolent	jurisprudence	mayhem
inert	knit	meander
ingenuous	laborious	memento
inherent	laceration	mendacious
innocuous	lackluster	metamorphosis
insensible	laconic	
insinuate	largess	
insipid	lassitude	
insularity	latent	
intractable	laud	
intransigence	lethargic	
inundate	levee	
inured	levity	
invective	lucid	
iota	magnanimity	

INCONGRUITY (n) *[in-kuh n-GROO-i-tee]*

Syn: lack of harmony; absurdity

Ant: sense; congruity

Usage: The *incongruity* and discrepancies in the two charts were very obvious.

INCONSEQUENTIAL (adj) *[in-kon-si-KWEN-shuh l]*

Syn: insignificant; unimportant

Ant: important; meaningful

Usage: One elderly woman's peaceful death in the city, at a time when it was being rocked by a hundred bombings every day, was but an *inconsequential* event.

INCORPORATE (v) *[in-KAWR-puh-reyt]*

Syn: introduce something into a larger whole; combine; unite

Ant: separate

Usage: We informed the director of the company that it would take a few weeks to *incorporate* his suggestions into the new system.

INDETERMINATE (adj) *[in-di-TUR-muh-nit]*

Syn: uncertain; not clearly fixed; indefinite

Ant: definite; clear

Usage: The consequences of the event are *indeterminate* as of now.

INDIGENCE (n) *[IN-di-juh ns]*

Syn: poverty

Ant: affluence

Usage: Moved by the *indigence* and poverty he came upon during his visit, the President pledged to set aside a major chunk of funds for community development.

(Incongruity – Metamorphosis)

Chapter 6

INDOLENT (adj) *[IN-dl-uh nt]*

Syn: lazy; like a couch potato

Ant: dynamic; energetic

Usage: He stretched out *indolently,* feeling too full of laziness to do anything productive on a Sunday.

INERT (adj) *[in-URT]*

Syn: inactive; lacking power to move

Ant: active

Usage: The dog was lying *inert* and still on the carpet when she opened the door.

INGENUOUS (adj) *[in-JEN-yoo-uh s]*

Syn: naïve and trusting; young; unsophisticated

Ant: disingenuous; sly; reserved; mean; insincere; crafty; cunning; urbane

Usage: The young lady is very naïve and *ingenuous.*

INHERENT (adj) *[in-HEER-uh nt]*

Syn: firmly established by nature or habit

Ant: acquired

Usage: His *inherent* honesty and diligence have stood him in good stead.

INNOCUOUS (adj) *[ih-NOK-yoo-uh s]*

Syn: harmless

Ant: hurtful; injurious; stimulating

Usage: Seemingly *innocuous* statements made by the president were contrived by the media to look sinister.

INSENSIBLE (adj) *[in-SEN-suh-buh l]*

Syn: unconscious; unresponsive; unaware; inconsiderate

Ant: feeling; caring; sensitive

Usage: It was an *insensible,* foolish act.

INSINUATE (v) *[in-SIN-yoo-eyt]*

Syn: hint; imply; creep in

Ant: state; affirm; propound; announce; withdraw; retract; extract

Usage: He didn't dare openly accuse Benedict, but he did *insinuate* that many a wrongdoing had been attributed to him.

INSIPID (adj) *[in-SIP-id]*

Syn: lacking in flavor; dull

Ant: racy; intense; strong; full-flavored; bright; sparkling

Usage: The *insipid* food was so bland even his dog refused to eat it.

INSULARITY (n) *[in-suh-LAR-i-tee]*

Syn: narrow-mindedness; isolation; xenophobia

Ant: open-mindedness

Usage: The *insularity* and narrow-mindedness of the community was growing each day.

INTRACTABLE (adj) *[in-TRAK-tuh-buh l]*

Syn: unruly; stubborn; unyielding

Ant: flexible; adaptable

Usage: At times, he can be *intractable* and obstinate to an annoying extent.

(Incongruity – Metamorphosis)

Chapter 6

INTRANSIGENCE (n) *[in-TRAN-si-juh ns]*

Syn: refusal of any compromise; stubbornness

Ant: inclination

Usage: Her *intransigence* and willfulness could someday bring her downfall.

INUNDATE (v) *[IN-uh n-deyt]*

Syn: overwhelm; flood; submerge

Ant: underwhelm

Usage: The town council's mailbox was *inundated* with complaints from the residents.

INURED (adj) *[in-YOO R d]*

Syn: accustomed; hardened

Ant: sensitive; tender

Usage: Circumstances and life's harsh battles had made him *inured* to pain.

INVECTIVE (n) *[in-VEK-tiv]*

Syn: abuse

Ant: commendation; eulogy; panegyric; laudation; praise; encouragement

Usage: We hadn't expected or anticipated that Patrick would deliver such *invective* in his restaurant critique.

IOTA (n) *[ahy-OH-tuh]*

Syn: very small quantity

Ant: large amount

Usage: He had not an *iota* of compassion in him as he kicked the wounded man with his hard boots.

IRASCIBLE (adj) *[i-RAS-uh-buh l]*

Syn: irritable; easily angered

Ant: courteous

Usage: Ken becomes *irascible* when someone talks about the war, hearing unspoken criticism because he didn't enlist.

IRREMEDIABLE (adj) *[ir-i-MEE-dee-uh-buh l]*

Syn: incurable; uncorrectable

Ant: correctable

Usage: The doctors gave up on her case saying it was an *irremediable*, hopeless situation and they could do nothing about it.

IRRESOLUTE (adj) *[i-REZ-uh-loot]*

Syn: uncertain how to act; weak

Ant: resolute; determined; bold; decided; firm; persistent

Usage: The jury returned with an *irresolute* verdict as they had not come to a firm decision.

ITINERARY (n) *[ahy-TIN-uh-RER-ee]*

Syn: plan of a trip

Usage: The *itinerary* for the ten-day tour to Europe had not yet been finalized.

JETTISON (v) *[JET-uh-suh n]*

Syn: throw overboard; eject

Ant: take on

Usage: With one unexpected move he *jettisoned* the castaway from the deck into the sea.

(Incongruity – Metamorphosis)

Chapter 6

JURISPRUDENCE (n) *[joo r-is-PROOD-ns]*

Syn: science of law

Usage: She decided to take up the major of *jurisprudence* to become a lawyer.

KNIT (v) *[nit]*

Syn: make a garment with knitting needles; contract into wrinkles; grow together

Usage: She had a wish to *knit* him a blue sweater.

LABORIOUS (adj) *[luh-BAWR-ee-uh s]*

Syn: demanding much work or care; tedious

Ant: idle; lazy; indolent; easy; light; simple

Usage: I was moved by his *laborious* efforts and paid him twenty dollars more than what I'd promised him.

LACERATION (n) *[las-uh-rey-shuhn]*

Syn: torn, ragged wound

Usage: He then dropped the heavy grinder onto his ankle, causing a severe *laceration*.

LACKLUSTER (adj) *[LAK-luhs-ter]*

Syn: dull; lifeless

Ant: ebullient; enthusiastic; lively

Usage: The bland and boring dinner was a *lackluster* affair.

LACONIC (adj) *[luh-KON-ik]*

Syn: brief and to the point

Ant: authoritarian; verbose; garrulous; loquacious; prosy; lengthy

Usage: His replies were *laconic* and terse, so his audience refrained from asking too many questions.

LARGESS (n) *[lahr-JES]*

Syn: generous gift; generosity

Ant: parsimony; stinginess; avarice

Usage: The old dowager loved to bestow her *largess* upon her poorer nieces.

LASSITUDE (n) *[LAS-i-tood]*

Syn: laziness; languor; weariness; lethargy

Ant: strength; activity; freshness

Usage: He was overcome by a feeling of lethargy and *lassitude* and was reluctant to even emerge from the bed.

LATENT (adj) *[LEYT-nt]*

Syn: potential but undeveloped; dormant; hidden

Ant: visible; apparent; manifest; conspicuous; explicit

Usage: The air between the man and the woman was *latent* with desire.

LAUD (adj) *[lawd]*

Syn: praise

Ant: decry; criticize

Usage: The ministers present at the swearing-in ceremony *lauded* the efforts of the newly elected senator.

LETHARGIC (adj) *[luh-THAHR-jik]*

Syn: drowsy; dull; sluggish

Ant: energetic

Usage: It was a chilly wintry morning and she felt more *lethargic* than ever in her warm bed.

LEVEE (n) *[LEV-ee]*

Syn: earthen or stone embankment to prevent flooding

Usage: Levees are usually built by piling earth on a cleared, level surface next to a waterway.

LEVITY (n) *[LEV-i-tee]*

Syn: lack of seriousness; lightness

Ant: gravity; earnestness; seriousness; sobriety

Usage: There was a lot of *levity* and merriment in the air at the annual holiday party.

LUCID (adj) *[LOO-sid]*

Syn: easily understood; clear; intelligible

Ant: muddied; unclear; foggy

Usage: The report was very clear and *lucid*, providing adequate information to make the decision.

MAGNANIMITY (n) *[mag-nuh-NIM-i-tee]*

Syn: generosity; kindness

Ant: selfishness; malevolence

Usage: The nuns were overwhelmed by his *magnanimity*; none had ever before given their orphanage such an enormous sum of money along with the huge bounties of clothes and toys.

MALIGN (v) *[muh-LAHYN]*

Syn: speak evil of; bad-mouth; defame

Ant: laud; praise

Usage: The business tycoon was publicly *maligned* by a former employee who claimed that he used to often ill-treat her and harass her.

MALINGERER (n) *[muh-LING-ger-er]*

Syn: one who feigns illness to escape duty; slacker; idler

Ant: go-getter; hard worker

Usage: Ken has acquired a reputation of sorts for being a *malingerer* and idler.

MALLEABLE (adj) *[MAL-ee-uh-buh l]*

Syn: capable of being shaped by pounding; impressionable

Ant: relentless

Usage: The politician has a very *malleable* personality and can easily switch from one mood to another.

MARTINET (n) *[mahr-tn-ET]*

Syn: strict disciplinarian; authoritarian

Ant: participative leader

Usage: Mr. Parker was a strict disciplinarian, a true *martinet*.

MAVERICK (n) *[MAV-er-ik]*

Syn: rebel; nonconformist; radical

Ant: conformist

Usage: Jonah is a *maverick,* preferring to travel the world and learn new things and do odd jobs than stay stuck to a desk job.

MAYHEM (n) *[MEY-hem]*

Syn: chaos; confusion; anarchy

(Incongruity – Metamorphosis)

Ant: calm; harmony; peace

Usage: There was chaos and *mayhem* at the stadium when the match was abruptly called off.

MEANDER (v) *[mee-AN-der]*

Syn: (of rivers and streams) to flow slowly along a winding course; wander

Ant: go direct

Usage: The dog was found *meandering* about the meadow.

MEMENTO (n) *[muh-MEN-toh]*

Syn: token; reminder

Usage: He treasured the silver *memento* presented to him at his farewell party for several years.

MENDACIOUS (adj) *[men-DEY-shuh s]*

Syn: lying; habitually dishonest

Ant: trustworthy

Usage: Her *mendacious* statements shocked him for their total lack of foundation in truth and reality.

METAMORPHOSIS (n) *[met-uh-MAWR-fuh-sis]*

Syn: change of form

Usage: She underwent a gradual *metamorphosis* and emerged a better person than she was before.

This page is intentionally left blank

Chapter 7

(Meticulous - Piety)

This chapter covers the following words along with their part of speech, pronunciation, synonyms and antonym, if applicable. Sample usage of the word is also illustrated.

meticulous
minuscule
misanthrope
mite
mitigate
mollify
morose
motif
mundane
negate
neophyte
nicety
notable
nuance
nuptial
obdurate
obscure
obsequious
obviate

occlude
officious
olfactory
omnipotent
onerous
opprobrium
oscillate
ostentatious
panoramic
paradox
paragon
paraphernalia
parched
parity
partisan
pathological
patriarch
paucity
pedantic

penance
penchant
penury
perennial
perfidious
perfunctory
permeable
personable
pervasive
perversion
phlegmatic
piety

METICULOUS (adj) *[muh-TIK-yuh-luh s]*

Syn: excessively careful

Ant: remiss; careless

Usage: Gary was *meticulous* in his efforts, careful to attend to every detail.

MINUSCULE (adj) *[MIN-uh-skyool]*

Syn: extremely small; diminutive

Ant: grand; large

Usage: The difference in the two rates is *miniscule,* having very little effect on the final outcome.

MISANTHROPE (n) *[MIS-uh n-throhp]*

Syn: one who hates mankind

Ant: philanthropist; humanitarian

Usage: Fred is known to be a *misanthrope*; he dislikes mingling with people or helping others in any way.

MITE (n) *[mahyt]*

Syn: very small object or creature; small coin; tiny piece; bit

Ant: whole

Usage: He didn't have a *mite* of compassion in him.

MITIGATE (v) *[mit-i-geyt]*

Syn: lessen in intensity; moderate

Ant: exacerbate

Usage: Can you do anything to *mitigate* the risk from another's business?

MOLLIFY (v) *[MOL-uh-fahy]*

Syn: soothe; appease

Ant: agitate; incite; provoke

Usage: We all tried to *mollify* her, but it was in vain; she would not be appeased.

MOROSE (adj) *[muh-ROHS]*

Syn: ill-humored; sullen; melancholy

Ant: genial; kindly; gentle; indulgent; joyous; merry; gay

Usage: I wanted to know why Karen looked so *morose* and sad.

MOTIF (n) *[moh-TEEF]*

Syn: theme; design

Usage: A floral *motif* has been a perennial favorite among fashion designers.

MUNDANE (adj) *[muhn-DEYN]*

Syn: worldly, as opposed to spiritual; boring; banal

Ant: exciting; extraordinary

Usage: Moira is planning to leave her current job because its *mundane* tasks bore her.

NEGATE (v) *[ni-GEYT]*

Syn: cancel out; nullify; deny; contradict

Ant: allow; approve; permit

Usage: This one misdeed *negated* all his charity.

NEOPHYTE (n) *[NEE-uh-fahyt]*

Syn: beginner; novice

Ant: expert

Usage: This movie features that *neophyte*. I wonder how well he has acted in his first lead role.

NICETY (n) *[NAHY-si-tee]*

Syn: detail; nuance; precision; minute distinction

Ant: generality; whole

Usage: It took more than three months of hosting parties for her to understand the *niceties* of serving food to the guests.

NOTABLE (adj) *[noh-tuh-buhl]*

Syn: conspicuous; important; distinguished; famous

Ant: inconspicuous; unimportant; commonplace; ordinary

Usage: Simon bought the antique Teddy Bear at an auction of stuffed animals in Cornwall, *notable* for the presence and enthusiastic bidding of Harry Hills.

NUANCE (n) *[NOO-ahns]*

Syn: shade of difference in meaning or color; subtle distinction

Ant: whole

Usage: Sheila agreed that she would need a few more years to understand the finer *nuances* of music.

NUPTIAL (adj) *[NUHP-shuh l]*

Syn: related to marriage

Usage: The tour guide showed us the exquisitely decorated *nuptial* chamber in the hundred-year-old palace.

OBDURATE (adj) *[OB-doo-rit]*

Syn: stubborn

Ant: flexible; amenable; docile; tractable

Usage: I wonder how he is going to convince the *obdurate* defenders of the status quo.

OBSCURE (v) *[uhb-skyoor]*

Syn: darken; make unclear

Ant: lighten; brighten; unveil; expose

Usage: The beautiful view was *obscured* by an ugly abandoned building.

OBSEQUIOUS (adj) *[uh b-SEE-kwee-uh s]*

Syn: slavishly attentive; servile; sycophantic

Ant: arrogant; assertive

Usage: Harold was totally *obsequious* to John till he learned that he was also a laborer and not a supervisor.

OBVIATE (v) *[OB-vee-eyt]*

Syn: make unnecessary; get rid of

Ant: necessitate; compel; order

Usage: In some fields, work experience *obviates* the need for a formal degree.

OCCLUDE (v) *[uh-KLOOD]*

Syn: shut; close; block

Ant: open; allow; permit

Usage: He *occluded* the passage by lining the entrance with thorns.

OFFICIOUS (adj) *[uh-FISH-uh s]*

Syn: meddlesome; excessively pushy in offering one's services; self-important; dictatorial

Ant: modest; retiring; negligent; timid

Usage: Sheila disliked *officious* interference from her family.

OLFACTORY (adj) *[ol-FAK-tuh-ree]*

Syn: concerning the sense of smell

Usage: Her *olfactory* sense is very sharp so she hates any bad odors lurking at home.

OMNIPOTENT (adj) *[om-NIP-uh-tuh nt]*

Syn: all-powerful

Ant: weak; ineffective; powerless

Usage: He hated to work in the shadow of his seemingly *omnipotent* boss.

ONEROUS (adj) *[ON-er-uh s]*

Syn: burdensome

Ant: light; easy; trivial; slight

Usage: It really was an *onerous* task managing the naughty puppies.

OPPROBRIUM (n) *[uh-PROH-bree-uh m]*

Syn: public shame; infamy; disgrace; scorn

Ant: honor; respect; glory; praise

Usage: The minister's misdeeds have attracted public *opprobrium*.

OSCILLATE (v) *[OS-uh-leyt]*

Syn: vibrate pendulum-like; waver

Ant: stand still

Usage: Sheila's moods keep *oscillating* between despair and joy.

OSTENTATIOUS (adj) *[os-ten-tey-shuh]*

Syn: showy; pretentious; trying to attract attention

Ant: unpretentious

Usage: Her friend's wedding reception was *ostentatious*, complete with swans and a seven-tiered cake.

PANORAMIC (adj) *[pan-uh-ram-ic]*

Syn: denoting an unobstructed and comprehensive view

Ant: limited; cropped

Usage: We then headed down to the indoor pool and slowly swam a few lengths while admiring the *panoramic* view through the huge picture windows.

PARADOX (n) *[PAR-uh-doks]*

Syn: something apparently contradictory in nature; a statement that looks false but is actually correct

Ant: harmony

Usage: The most efficient employee in this organization is the least educated… what a *paradox*!

PARAGON (n) *[PAR-uh-gon]*

Syn: model of perfection

Ant: worst example

Usage: She was not a *paragon* of virtue, but she was both kind and chaste.

PARAPHERNALIA (n) *[par-uh-fer-NEYL-yuh]*

Syn: equipment; odds and ends

Usage: The plumber arrived with all the *paraphernalia* for repairing the water pump.

PARCHED (adj) *[pahrch d]*

Syn: extremely dry; very thirsty

Ant: damp; moist; quenched

Usage: She was *parched* after the long walk in the sweltering afternoon heat.

PARITY (n) *[PAR-i-tee]*

Syn: equality; close resemblance

Ant: disparity; inequality

Usage: She was happy that there was *parity* between the work she did and the wages she was paid.

PARTISAN (adj) *[PAHR-tuh-zuh n]*

Syn: one-sided; prejudiced; committed to a party

Ant: independent

Usage: Having a *partisan* referee is the same as having none.

PATHOLOGICAL (adj) *[path-uh-LOJ-i-kuh l]*

Syn: pertaining to disease; morbid

Ant: healthy

Usage: He suffers from an almost *pathological* fear of darkness.

PATRIARCH (n) *[PEY-tree-ahrk]*

Syn: father and ruler of a family or tribe

Ant: matriarch

Usage: It was very clear that Mr. Diaz was the *patriarch* of the family; there was no opposing him.

Chapter 7

PAUCITY (n) *[PAW-si-tee]*

Syn: scarcity; dearth

Ant: plenty

Usage: There was a *paucity* of imagination in the author's first dry and lifeless novel.

PEDANTIC (adj) *[puh-DAN-tik]*

Syn: showing off learning; bookish

Ant: modest

Usage: His lecture was so *pedantic* and uninteresting.

PENANCE (n) *[PEN-uh ns]*

Syn: self-imposed punishment for sin; regret; contrition

Ant: indifference; meanness

Usage: His lifestyle has become one of fasting, *penance,* and pilgrimage, all to atone for the fatal accident she caused.

PENCHANT (n) *[PEN-chuh nt]*

Syn: strong inclination; liking

Ant: dislike; indifference; hatred

Usage: She has a *penchant* for collecting antique utensils.

PENURY (n) *[PEN-yuh-ree]*

Syn: severe poverty; stinginess

Ant: wealth; affluence

Usage: He was brought up in *penury*, with no formal education, poor healthcare, and limited prospects.

PERENNIAL (n) *[puh-REN-ee-uh l]*

Syn: something that is continuing or recurrent; an everlasting plant

Ant: annual (plant)

Usage: This species is a low-growing *perennial*, brightening our yard year after year.

PERFIDIOUS (adj) *[per-FID-ee-uh s]*

Syn: treacherous; disloyal

Ant: staunch; faithful; honorable

Usage: She could never forgive her *perfidious* team members for their treachery.

PERFUNCTORY (adj) *[per-FUHNGK-tuh-ree]*

Syn: superficial; not thorough; lacking interest, care, or enthusiasm

Ant: heedful; careful; thoughtful; caring

Usage: I was disappointed to be greeted with no more than a *perfunctory* handshake.

PERMEABLE (adj) *[PUR-mee-uh-buh l]*

Syn: penetrable; porous; allowing liquids or gas to pass through

Ant: impermeable; solid

Usage: Most clothing items are *permeable* to air and water, letting either through to the skin with just a short exposure.

PERSONABLE (adj) *[PUR-suh-nuh-buh l]*

Syn: attractive

Ant: disagreeable

Usage: The people I met at the conference were intelligent and *personable*.

PERVASIVE (adj) *[per-VEY-siv]*

Syn: pervading; spread throughout (as an attitude)

Ant: contained; limited; narrow

Usage: Ronnie lives with a *pervasive* sense of guilt invading his every thought.

PERVERSION (n) *[per-VUR-zhuh n]*

Syn: corruption; turning from right to wrong; sexual deviance

Ant: merit; honor; valor; decency

Usage: I wonder what *perversion* of the mind caused him to bomb a bus carrying so many children.

PHLEGMATIC (adj) *[fleg-MAT-ik]*

Syn: calm; not easily disturbed; unemotional

Ant: passionate; active; energetic; interested; alert; restless

Usage: Looking out of the window, I saw a *phlegmatic* man sweeping the sidewalk despite the heavy rain.

PIETY (n) *[PAHY-i-tee]*

Syn: religious devotion; godliness

Ant: impiety; ungodliness; profanity; hypocrisy; irreverence

Usage: Her *piety* has gained her the respect of her church and the entire neighborhood.

This page is intentionally left blank

Chapter 8

(Pious - Redolent)

This chapter covers the following words along with their part of speech, pronunciation, synonyms and antonym, if applicable. Sample usage of the word is also illustrated.

- pious
- placate
- platitude
- plethora
- plumage
- plummet
- porous
- posterity
- postulate
- practicable
- pragmatic
- pragmatist
- preamble
- precedent
- precipitate
- preclude
- precocious
- precursor
- premonitory
- preposterous
- presentiment
- presumptuous
- prevaricate
- pristine
- problematic
- prodigal
- profound
- prognosticate
- prohibitive
- proliferate
- propellants
- propensity
- propinquity
- propitiate
- propriety
- proscenium
- proscribe
- prudent
- pseudonym
- psychosis
- pulmonary
- qualified
- quibble
- quiescent
- rarefied
- recalcitrant
- recant
- recluse
- recondite
- redolent

PIOUS (adj) *[PAHY-uh s]*

Syn: devout; religious

Ant: ungodly; sinful; hypocritical; bad

Usage: His attitude is truly compassionate throughout the community, not just a *pious* front within the church.

PLACATE (v) *[PLEY-keyt]*

Syn: pacify; conciliate

Ant: snub

Usage: Betty smiled and spoke sweetly, trying to *placate* John after their heated argument.

PLATITUDE (n) *[PLAT-i-tood]*

Syn: trite remark; commonplace statement

Ant: originality

Usage: It is boring to listen to him spouting the same old *platitudes*.

PLETHORA (n) *[PLETH-er-uh]*

Syn: excess; overabundance

Ant: paucity; dearth

Usage: A *plethora* of imported appliances are available in the market.

PLUMAGE (n) *[ploo-mij]*

Syn: feathers of birds

Usage: The illustrated birdwatcher's guide contains many plates showing most *plumage* variations as well as useful text and maps.

Chapter 8

PLUMMET (v) *[PLUHM-it]*

Syn: fall sharply

Ant: ascend; rise; shoot up; skyrocket

Usage: Share prices in the stock market have *plummeted* for the third consecutive day, with many investors fearing continuing drops.

POROUS (adj) *[PAWR-uh s]*

Syn: full of pores; like a sieve

Ant: solid; nonporous; impervious

Usage: The water seeped through the *porous* limestone.

POSTERITY (n) *[po-STER-i-tee]*

Syn: descendants; future generations

Ant: forebears

Usage: The photos in the album are being preserved for *posterity*.

POSTULATE (n) *[POS-chuh-lit]*

Syn: semi-evident truth; theory

Ant: fact

Usage: His idea became the *postulate* for many further arguments in the subject.

PRACTICABLE (adj) *[PRAK-ti-kuh-buh l]*

Syn: feasible; possible; practical

Ant: impractical; impossible; unattainable

Usage: The manager is very popular because his plans are all *practicable*.

PRAGMATIC (adj) [prag-MAT-ik]

Syn: practical (as opposed to idealistic); concerned with the practical worth or impact of something

Ant: impractical; idealistic; unrealistic

Usage: Robin took a very *pragmatic* look at her situation, ready to start the necessary steps forward toward a workable solution.

PRAGMATIST (n) [PRAG-muh-tist]

Syn: practical person

Ant: idealist

Usage: Her handling of the problem showed that she was a *pragmatist*, wanting to get to the underlying causes and quickly move forward to a solution.

PREAMBLE (n) [PREE-am-buh l]

Syn: introductory statement

Ant: peroration; finale; conclusion; essay; body

Usage: Rather than a brief introduction, the *preamble* turned out to last longer than the speech!

PRECEDENT (n) [pres-i-duh-nt]

Syn: something preceding in time that may be used as an authority or guide for future action; antecedent

Ant: result

Usage: This court decision sets a *precedent* for future cases of a similar nature.

PRECIPITATE (adj) [pri-SIP-i-tit]

Syn: rash; premature; hasty; sudden

Ant: deliberate; slow; shallow; inclined

Chapter 8

Usage: The manager advised his team not to make *precipitate* decisions and instead gather more data.

PRECLUDE (v) *[pri-KLOOD]*

Syn: make impossible; eliminate; prevent

Ant: admit; promote; further; advance

Usage: He evaded questions in order to *preclude* any further discussion.

PRECOCIOUS (adj) *[pri-KOH-shuh s]*

Syn: advanced in development

Ant: delayed; stunted

Usage: She has a *precocious* talent for music, playing Bach sonatas at the age of six.

PRECURSOR (n) *[pri-KUR-ser]*

Syn: forerunner; antecedent; harbinger

Ant: sequel; descendent

Usage: The media is publicizing the deal as a *precursor* to a merger; investors are acting quickly before the final deal is sealed.

PREMONITORY (adj) *[pri-MON-i-tawr-ee]*

Syn: serving to warn; foreboding; menacing

Ant: auspicious; promising; propitious

Usage: She is afraid last night's dream may be a *premonitory* one, predicting a bleak future.

PREPOSTEROUS (adj) *[pri-POS-ter-uh s]*

Syn: absurd; ridiculous

Ant: reasonable; moderate; sound; right

Usage: I wonder who suggested that *preposterous* idea; it's far beyond anything we would ever consider.

PRESENTIMENT (n) *[pri-ZEN-tuh-muh nt]*

Syn: feeling something will happen; anticipatory fear; premonition

Ant: surprise; miscalculation; accident; foreknowledge

Usage: Betty had a *presentiment* that some disaster would befall her during that fateful journey.

PRESUMPTUOUS (adj) *[pri-ZUHMP-choo-uh s]*

Syn: arrogant; taking liberties

Ant: modest; diffident; bashful; hesitating; unassuming

Usage: It was very *presumptuous* of him to advise me regarding my private affairs.

PREVARICATE (v) *[pri-VAR-i-keyt]*

Syn: lie

Ant: affirm; maintain; prove; substantiate

Usage: The ministers continued to *prevaricate* despite the public queries about their truthfulness.

PRISTINE (adj) *[PRIS-teen]*

Syn: characteristic of earlier times; primitive; unspoiled

Ant: spoiled; polluted; dirty

Usage: He is always dressed in *pristine* white shirts, without a spot on them.

PROBLEMATIC (adj) *[prob-luh-MAT-ik]*

Syn: doubtful; unsettled; questionable; perplexing

Ant: certain; settled; solvable

Usage: Roderick is a very *problematic* child, resulting in daily complaints from his teachers.

PRODIGAL (adj) *[PROD-i-guh l]*

Syn: wasteful; reckless with money; extravagant

Ant: frugal; economical; close; saving; miserly; stingy

Usage: If she continues her *prodigal* habits, she'll end up in the poorhouse someday.

PROFOUND (adj) *[pruh-FOUND]*

Syn: deep; not superficial; complete

Ant: shallow; superficial; slight

Usage: She displays a *profound* understanding of the subject, able to answer any question from the audience.

PROGNOSTICATE (v) *[prog-NOS-ti-keyt]*

Syn: predict; foretell

Ant: ignore

Usage: It is difficult to *prognosticate* about the future of this company.

PROHIBITIVE (adj) *[proh-HIB-i-tiv]*

Syn: extremely high (of prices etc.); restrictive

Ant: reasonable; unlimited

Usage: The cost of building a house was so *prohibitive* that he decided to continue renting instead.

PROLIFERATE (v) *[pruh-LIF-uh-reyt]*

Syn: grow rapidly; spread; multiply

Ant: decline; decrease; limit

Usage: In his speech, the President condemned the *proliferation* of nuclear weapons, urging instead a mutual arms reduction.

PROPELLANTS (n) *[pruh-pel-uhnts]*

Syn: substances that propel or drive forward; explosives

Ant: hindrance

Usage: Avoid buying aerosols that use CFCs as *propellants* for their sprays.

PROPENSITY (n) *[pruh-PEN-si-tee]*

Syn: natural inclination

Ant: aversion; disinclination; indisposition

Usage: It didn't take long to realize her *propensity* to lie; not a single word of truth crossed her lips!

PROPINQUITY (n) *[proh-PING-kwi-tee]*

Syn: nearness; kinship

Ant: distance

Usage: The *propinquity* of his home and office is a great advantage for him, especially with rising fuel prices.

PROPITIATE (v) *[pruh-PISH-ee-eyt]*

Syn: appease

Ant: alienate; estrange; exasperate

Usage: Betty always went out of the way to *propitiate* people, explaining why he has few friends.

PROPRIETY (n) *[pruh-PRAHY-i-tee]*

Syn: fitness; correct conduct

Ant: impropriety; misbehavior

Usage: He behaved with absolutely no sense of social *propriety*, to the great consternation of the other guests at the party.

PROSCENIUM (n) *[proh-SEE-nee-uh m]*

Syn: a stage in front of curtain

Ant: backstage

Usage: Barbara rushed to the *proscenium* as soon as the play was over to congratulate the artists.

PROSCRIBE (v) *[proh-SKRAHYB]*

Syn: ostracize; banish; outlaw

Ant: prescribe; allow

Usage: In many countries members of the general public are *proscribed* from owning guns.

PRUDENT (adj) *[PROOD-nt]*

Syn: cautious; careful; timid

Ant: temerarious; reckless; adventurous

Usage: I suggest you adopt a *prudent* approach to solving this problem lest rash behavior make the situation even worse!

PSEUDONYM (n) *[SOOD-n-im]*

Syn: pen name; alias

Ant: actual name

Usage: She writes all her mystery novels under the *pseudonym* Sharp rather than her true surname of Smith.

PSYCHOSIS (n) *[sahy-KOH-sis]*

Syn: mental disorder

Ant: mental health

Usage: Her psychiatrist has diagnosed her problem to be *psychosis,* with recurring bouts of depression.

PULMONARY (adj) *[puhl-muh-ner-ee]*

Syn: pertaining to the lungs

Usage: The only thing doctors could do was balloon the stent in his *pulmonary* artery.

QUALIFIED (adj) *[KWOL-uh-fahyd]*

Syn: limited; restricted (secondary meaning)

Ant: incompetent; ineligible

Usage: My son is a *qualified* physician with his new license to practice proudly displayed on his office wall.

QUIBBLE (n) *[KWIB-uh l]*

Syn: minor objection or complaint

Ant: major argument

Usage: Rob and his brother decided to forget their past *quibbles* and shook hands in friendship.

QUIESCENT (adj) *[kwee-ES-uh nt]*

Syn: at rest; dormant; temporarily inactive; motionless; still

Ant: active; excited

Usage: She chose a *quiescent* beach resort instead of a popular and crowded one.

RAREFIED (adj) *[RAIR-uh-fahyd]*

Syn: made less dense [of a gas]

Ant: concentrated

Usage: Astronauts cannot adjust to the *rarefied* atmosphere of outer space, so they breathe concentrated air from their survival tanks.

RECALCITRANT (adj) *[ri-KAL-si-truh nt]*

Syn: obstinately stubborn; determined to resist authority; unruly

Ant: hospitable

Usage: He can coax even the most *recalcitrant* employee to put in his best efforts.

RECANT (v) *[ri-KANT]*

Syn: disclaim or disavow; retract a previous statement; openly confess error

Ant: propound; assert; maintain; declare; hold

Usage: He was forced to *recant* his heresy and instead pledge allegiance to the church.

RECLUSE (n) *[REK-loos]*

Syn: hermit; loner

Ant: extrovert

Usage: His widow became a virtual *recluse* for the rest of her life, rarely stepping beyond her garden fence.

RECONDITE (adj) *[REK-uh n-dahyt]*

Syn: (of ideas, knowledge, etc.) not commonly known; difficult to understand; profound; abstruse

Ant: obvious; simple; straightforward

Usage: I wonder how she manages to understand even *recondite* subject matter with ease.

REDOLENT (adj) *[RED-l-uh nt]*

Syn: fragrant; odorous; suggestive of an odor

Ant: noxious; putrid; stinking

Usage: Her garden was *redolent* with the pleasant scent of rosemary.

Chapter 9

(Refractory - Supersede)

This chapter covers the following words along with their part of speech, pronunciation, synonyms and antonym, if applicable. Sample usage of the word is also illustrated.

refractory	scrupulous	stolid
refute	seasoned	striated
relegate	secrete	strut
remunerative	sedentary	strut
replete	sedition	submissive
reproach	seemly	subpoena
reprobate	seep	subside
repudiate	serenity	substantiate
residue	shard	sumptuous
resolution	skeptic	supersede
resolve	sluice	
reverent	sodden	
rue	solicitous	
ruse	soporific	
sage	specious	
salubrious	spectrum	
sanction	sporadic	
satiate	stigma	
saturate	stint	
savor	stipulate	

REFRACTORY (adj) *[ri-FRAK-tuh-ree]*

Syn: stubborn; unmanageable

Ant: manageable; obedient

Usage: No amount of reprimanding could control the *refractory* laborers.

REFUTE (v) *[ri-FYOOT]*

Syn: disprove

Ant: prove; confirm; establish; affirm; accept

Usage: Her arguments are so logical that it is impossible to *refute* them.

RELEGATE (v) *[REL-i-geyt]*

Syn: banish to an inferior position; delegate; assign

Ant: promote; elevate

Usage: After a few days, the newspapers *relegated* the old news item to the middle pages.

REMUNERATIVE (adj) *[ri-MYOO-ner-uh-tiv]*

Syn: compensating; rewarding; profitable

Ant: unprofitable

Usage: After winning the lottery, she left her *remunerative* job and volunteered at the old-age home.

REPLETE (adj) *[ri-PLEET]*

Syn: filled to the brim or to the paint of being stuffed; abundantly supplied

Ant: deficient; wanting; needy

Usage: With the pantry of the shelter *replete* with canned goods, the family was ready for the arrival of the intense storm and its expected aftermath of power outages.

Chapter 9

REPROACH (v) *[ri-PROHCH]*

Syn: express disapproval or disappointment

Ant: approve; extol; laud

Usage: She *reproached* him for breaking his promise.

REPROBATE (n) *[REP-ruh-beyt]*

Syn: person hardened in sin; devoid of a sense of decency

Ant: paragon

Usage: He has turned out exactly like his father, a drunken *reprobate*.

REPUDIATE (v) *[ri-PYOO-dee-eyt]*

Syn: disown; disavow

Ant: acknowledge; avow; admit

Usage: The media urged people to turn out in large numbers to *repudiate* the violence.

RESIDUE (n) *[REZ-i-doo]*

Syn: remainder; balance

Ant: whole

Usage: The explosion left a dusty *residue* on her skin.

RESOLUTION (n) *[rez-uh-LOO-shuh n]*

Syn: determination; resolve

Ant: indecision; composition; synthesis; inconsistency

Usage: She broke her New Year's *resolution* even before the end of January.

RESOLVE (n) *[ri-ZOLV]*

Syn: determination; firmness of purpose

Ant: indecision; uncertainty; lack of will

Usage: With that kind of firm *resolve,* she is sure to win.

REVERENT (adj) *[REV-er-uh nt]*

Syn: respectful; worshipful

Ant: irreverent

Usage: There was a *reverent* silence as the Principal entered the assembly hall.

RUE (v) *[roo]*

Syn: regret; lament; mourn

Ant: celebrate

Usage: She will *rue* the day she ever walked into my restaurant and criticized the food!

RUSE (n) *[rooz]*

Syn: trick; stratagem

Ant: overt act

Usage: It is now clear that this was a *ruse* to split up the two friends.

SAGE (n) *[seyj]*

Syn: person celebrated for wisdom

Ant: ignoramus; idiot

Usage: Ruth was inspired by the many stories she had read about ancient Chinese *sages* knowledgeable of complex subjects.

SALUBRIOUS (adj) *[suh-LOO-bree-uh s]*

Syn: healthful

Ant: unhealthy; unwholesome

(Refractory – Supersede)

Chapter 9

Usage: She enjoyed her stay at the *salubrious* hillside resort, welcoming the opportunity to heal her battered soul.

SANCTION (v) *[SANGK-shuh n]*

Syn: approve; ratify

Ant: discountenance; disallow; prohibit; nullify; disapprove; oppose

Usage: The manager *sanctioned* leave for his secretary so she could take a much-deserved vacation.

SATIATE (v) *[SEY-shee-eyt]*

Syn: satisfy fully

Ant: stint; starve

Usage: There are enough apples on the tree to *satiate* all the children in the neighborhood.

SATURATE (v) *[SACH-uh-reyt]*

Syn: soak thoroughly

Ant: drain; empty; dry; dilute

Usage: The market is *saturated* with imported goods.

SAVOR (v) *[sey-ver]*

Syn: enjoy; have a distinctive flavor, smell or quality

Ant: dislike; refuse; shun

Usage: She *savored* the flavor of each delicious mouthful as she ate.

SCRUPULOUS (adj) *[SKROO-pyuh-luh s]*

Syn: conscientious; extremely thorough

Ant: reckless; slovenly; confident; self-complacent

Usage: I have been *scrupulous* about telling them the risks associated with the venture.

SEASONED (adj) *[see-zuhn d]*

Syn: experienced; accomplished

Ant: inexperienced; unskilled

Usage: The manager was looking for a *seasoned* employee to lead the project team since the task was quite challenging.

SECRETE (v) *[si-KREET]*

Syn: hide away; produce and release a substance into an organism

Ant: publicize; absorb

Usage: The sweat glands *secrete* water and body waste.

SEDENTARY (adj) *[SED-n-ter-ee]*

Syn: requiring sitting; inactive

Ant: active; standing; mobile

Usage: A *sedentary* lifestyle has been linked with an increased risk of heart disease.

SEDITION (n) *[si-DISH-uh n]*

Syn: resistance to authority; insubordination

Ant: union; allegiance; obedience; order

Usage: Government officials charged him with *sedition* for has active opposition to the recently enacted law.

SEEMLY (adj) *[SEEM-lee]*

Syn: proper; appropriate

Ant: unbecoming; unsuitable; improper; indecent; incongruous

Usage: It was not *seemly* to allow a young school girl to go to the party unaccompanied.

SEEP (v) *[seep]*

Syn: ooze; trickle

Ant: flood; overwhelm

Usage: We dug retention ponds to allow rain water to *seep* back into the ground.

SERENITY (n) *[suh-REN-i-tee]*

Syn: calmness; placidity

Ant: chaos; excitability; stress

Usage: The monastery imparts a wonderful feeling of peace and *serenity*.

SHARD (n) *[shahrd]*

Syn: fragment, generally of pottery; small sample

Ant: whole

Usage: She wept over the *shards* of the heirloom vase that he had broken during the fight.

SKEPTIC (n) *[SKEP-tik]*

Syn: doubter; person who suspends judgment until the evidence supporting a point of view has been examined

Ant: believer; proponent

Usage: It's going to be difficult convincing the *skeptics* to approve his plans.

SLUICE (n) *[sloos]*

Syn: artificial channel for directing or controlling the flow of water

Usage: It's interesting to watch the water gush out of the *sluice* as soon as the gate is opened.

SODDEN (adj) *[SOD-n]*

Syn: soaked; dull, as if from drink

Ant: dry; abstinent

Usage: We stripped off our *sodden* shoes before entering the house.

SOLICITOUS (adj) *[suh-LIS-i-tuh s]*

Syn: worried; concerned

Ant: carefree; inconsiderate

Usage: He was so *solicitous* of his guests, anticipating their every need.

SOPORIFIC (adj) *[sop-uh-RIF-ik]*

Syn: sleep-causing; marked by sleepiness

Ant: stimulating; invigorating

Usage: Bob did not know what he was blabbering while under the *soporific* effects of the alcohol.

SPECIOUS (adj) *[SPEE-shuh s]*

Syn: seemingly reasonable but incorrect; misleading (often intentionally)

Ant: genuine

Usage: Duke was not convinced by her *specious* arguments; he still doubted her intentions.

Chapter 9

SPECTRUM (n) *[SPEK-truh m]*

Syn: colored band produced when a beam of light passes through a prism; variety

Usage: The broad *spectrum* of courses for students to choose from offers something for everyone.

SPORADIC (adj) *[spuh-RAD-ik]*

Syn: occurring irregularly

Ant: general; prevalent; continuous

Usage: The sound of *sporadic* shooting could still be heard at intervals through the night.

STIGMA (n) *[STIG-muh]*

Syn: token of disgrace; brand

Ant: decoration; laurels; credit; renown

Usage: There is still a meaningless *stigma* attached to certain professions like acting, relegating them to lower levels of respect.

STINT (v) *[stint]*

Syn: be thrifty; set limits; economize

Ant: lavish; pour; heap; squander

Usage: The chef advised his assistant not to *stint* on garnish in order to give the dish plenty of visual appeal.

STIPULATE (v) *[STIP-yuh-leyt]*

Syn: make express conditions; specify

Ant: retract; decline; refuse; withdraw; disagree

Usage: The match rules *stipulate* the number of extra golf clubs they can carry in their bags.

STOLID (adj) *[STOL-id]*

Syn: dull; impassive

Ant: acute; quick; clever; bright; sensitive

Usage: He looked up at the *stolid* face of the doctor, unable to determine whether the diagnosis was good or bad.

STRIATED (adj) *[STRAHY-ey-tid]*

Syn: marked with parallel bands; grooved

Ant: smooth; solid

Usage: The geologist studied the *striated* rock to learn from its bands more about the history of the region.

STRUT (n) *[struht]*

Syn: pompous walk; swagger

Ant: cower; retreat

Usage: Robert's confident *strut* in his graduation gown, waving his degree scroll, indicated his pride.

STRUT (n) *[struht]*

Syn: supporting bar (secondary meaning)

Usage: The architect designed the main *strut* to support loads from wind, snow, people, and the building itself.

SUBMISSIVE (adj) *[suh b-MIS-iv]*

Syn: yielding; timid; gentle

Ant: tenacious; brave

Usage: Zoya was anything but *submissive*; she would never give in to any circumstances or orders.

Chapter 9

SUBPOENA (n) *[suh-PEE-nuh]*

Syn: writ summoning a witness to appear; warrant; mandate

Usage: The entire staff of the company was served *subpoenas* to appear as witnesses for the prosecution.

SUBSIDE (v) *[suh b-SAHYD]*

Syn: settle down; descend; grow quiet

Ant: energize; increase; activate

Usage: After he took heavy medication the pain began to *subside*, allowing him to sleep peacefully.

SUBSTANTIATE (v) *[suh b-STAN-shee-eyt]*

Syn: establish by evidence; verify; support

Ant: contradict; disprove

Usage: The evidence was too meager and trivial to *substantiate* the charges.

SUMPTUOUS (adj) *[suhmp-choo-uh s]*

Syn: lavish; rich

Ant: poor; mean; inexpensive; sordid; beggarly; frugal

Usage: A large, *sumptuous* feast was laid out for them in the garden.

SUPERSEDE (v) *[soo-per-SEED]*

Syn: cause to be set aside; replace; make obsolete

Ant: confirm; perpetuate; continue; supply

Usage: The new dress code policy *superseded* the earlier one.

This page is intentionally left blank

Chapter 10

(Supposition - Yeoman)

This chapter covers the following words along with their part of speech, pronunciation, synonyms and antonym, if applicable. Sample usage of the word is also illustrated.

supposition	truncate	yeoman
tacit	tutelary	
tangential	unbridled	
tantamount	unwonted	
taut	vacillate	
tawdry	vapid	
tenuous	veneer	
testy	venerate	
tirade	venial	
titanic	veracious	
toga	verbose	
torpor	viable	
torso	vitreous	
tortuous	vituperative	
tractable	volatile	
transgression	warranted	
transient	wary	
transitoriness	welter	
truculence	whimsical	
truism	xenophobia	

SUPPOSITION (n) *[suhp-uh-ZISH-uh n]*

Syn: hypothesis; the act of supposing

Ant: proof

Usage: It was a mere *supposition* on his part; he had no proof to support his guesswork.

TACIT (adj) *[TAS-it]*

Syn: understood; not put into words

Ant: open; avowed; declared; expressed

Usage: The husband and wife had a remarkable *tacit* understanding between themselves, sometimes making words unnecessary.

TANGENTIAL (adj) *[tan-JEN-shuh l]*

Syn: peripheral; only slightly connected; digressing

Ant: core; critical

Usage: The bullet had hit the door in a *tangential* shot, chipping off a scant millimeter of wood.

TANTAMOUNT (adj) *[TAN-tuh-mount]*

Syn: equivalent in force, effect, or value

Ant: different; opposite; reverse

Usage: His action, though small, was *tantamount* to sacrilege and the elders rebuked him for it.

TAUT (adj) *[tawt]*

Syn: tight; ready

Ant: loose

Usage: He tied one last *taut* knot thus securing the bundle tightly around the bike, and then set off on the road for the long journey.

Chapter 10

TAWDRY (adj) *[TAW-dree]*

Syn: cheap and gaudy

Ant: tasteful

Usage: She was attired in a garish, *tawdry* manner, embarrassing the gentleman who had come to pick her up.

TENUOUS (adj) *[TEN-yoo-uh s]*

Syn: weak; very thin; slim

Ant: firm; strong

Usage: The mental patient had a *tenuous* grip on reality, often escaping to his world of fantasy.

TESTY (adj) *[TES-tee]*

Syn: irritable; short-tempered

Ant: good-humored

Usage: His mood was *testy* and irritable; it was best not to provoke him now.

TIRADE (n) *[TAHY-reyd]*

Syn: a long, angry, scolding speech; denunciation; harangue; outburst

Ant: calm; harmony; peace

Usage: The woman then launched into a lengthy *tirade* against him, listing out all his recent failures and mishaps.

TITANIC (adj) *[tahy-TAN-ik]*

Syn: gigantic; enormous

Ant: minuscule

Usage: The freighter was built of *titanic* proportions, looked huge and colossal, just waiting to conquer the seas.

TOGA (n) *[TOH-guh]*

Syn: Roman outer robe

Usage: For the drama on Saturday, Julian has had a silk *toga* made to suit his part as the Roman Emperor.

TORPOR (n) *[TAWR-per]*

Syn: lethargy; sluggishness; dormancy; apathy; inactivity

Ant: excitement; activity

Usage: She tried hard to wake him from his *torpor* and get him to do some chores, but he was feeling too lethargic and languid, so he resisted all her efforts.

TORSO (n) *[TAWR-soh]*

Syn: trunk of statue with head and limbs missing; human trunk

Usage: The farmboy had a lean, strong *torso* and didn't hesitate to show it off in front of the city-bred folks.

TORTUOUS (adj) *[TAWR-choo-uh s]*

Syn: winding; full of curves

Ant: straight; direct

Usage: The route was a very twisted, *tortuous* one through the mountains.

TRACTABLE (adj) *[TRAK-tuh-buh l]*

Syn: docile; easily managed

Ant: refractory; unmanageable; intractable; obstinate; stubborn

Usage: The new class seemed *tractable* so the teacher looked forward to the year, anticipating fewer discipline problems than in prior years.

Chapter 10

TRANSGRESSION (n) *[trans-GRESH-uh n]*

Syn: violation of a law; sin

Ant: upholding of a law; abidance

Usage: For his unwisely *transgression*, Paul was convicted and sentenced to a year's imprisonment.

TRANSIENT (adj) *[TRAN-shuh nt]*

Syn: momentary; temporary; staying for a short rime

Ant: permanent; lasting; abiding; perpetual; enduring

Usage: The *transient* pleasures offered by the hookah in the tent didn't seem particularly inviting to George.

TRANSITORINESS (n) *[TRAN-si-tawr-ee-nis]*

Syn: impermanence; brevity

Ant: permanence; longevity

Usage: The *transitoriness* of life sometimes depressed him to no end; he wished for immortality instead.

TRUCULENCE (n) *[TRUHK-yuh-luh ns]*

Syn: aggressiveness; ferocity

Ant: passivity; cowardice

Usage: The fierce sense of *truculence* he exhibited at such a young age alarmed his parents, fearful of many schoolyard fistfights in the future.

TRUISM (n) *[TROO-iz-uh m]*

Syn: self-evident truth; axiom; platitude

Ant: nonsense

Usage: He has a habit of collecting *truisms* like some people like to collect rare stamps.

TRUNCATE (v) *[TRUHNG-keyt]*

Syn: cut the top or end off

Ant: keep whole

Usage: The final words of the last paragraph had been *truncated* due to lack of space.

TUTELARY (adj) *[TOOT-l-er-ee]*

Syn: protective; pertaining to a guardianship

Ant: protected

Usage: His timely *tutelary* guidance was what led her to be such a successful dancer.

UNBRIDLED (adj) *[uhn-BRAHYD-ld]*

Syn: violent; unbounded

Ant: austere; severe; ascetic; virtuous; self-controlled; restrained

Usage: His *unbridled* optimism was infectious; others on the team began to expand their confidence that they could win.

UNWONTED (adj) *[uhn-WAWN-tid]*

Syn: unaccustomed; unusual

Ant: normal; regular

Usage: The *unwonted* kindness of strangers inspired the escaped convict to change his ways.

VACILLATE (v) *[VAS-uh-leyt]*

Syn: waver; fluctuate

Ant: remain constant

Usage: She tended to *vacillate* between two options and took a long time, if ever, to reach a conclusive decision.

(Supposition – Yeoman)

Chapter 10

VAPID (adj) *[VAP-id]*

Syn: dull and unimaginative; insipid and flavorless

Ant: inspiring

Usage: The critic declared the play totally *vapid*, a complete bore for everyone in the audience.

VENEER (n) *[vuh-NEER]*

Syn: thin layer; cover

Ant: entirety; depth

Usage: His suave charm was merely a *veneer* for his malicious inner nature.

VENERATE (v) *[VEN-uh-reyt]*

Syn: revere

Ant: scorn; disparage

Usage: Several tribes in the Mayan civilization *venerated* elements of nature as their deities.

VENIAL (adj) *[VEE-nee-uh l]*

Syn: forgivable; trivial

Ant: unpardonable; mortal; inexcusable; grave; serious

Usage: Since she was a newcomer and the mistake she had made was *venial*, she was easily forgiven by the rest of the group.

VERACIOUS (adj) *[vuh-REY-shuh s]*

Syn: truthful

Ant: deceitful; imaginary; fictional; fraudulent; lying; untrue

Usage: What they liked best about him was his truthful, *veracious* nature.

VERBOSE (adj) *[ver-BOHS]*

Syn: wordy; loquacious

Ant: succinct; terse

Usage: He is not normally this *verbose*; perhaps the drinks have made him open up.

VIABLE (adj) *[VAHY-uh-buh l]*

Syn: practical or workable; feasible; capable of maintaining life

Ant: impractical; impossible

Usage: The venture seemed like a *viable* proposition so they decided to sign the contract.

VITREOUS (adj) *[VI-tree-uh s]*

Syn: pertaining to or resembling glass; fragile

Ant: durable; flexible; resilient

Usage: The blue *vitreous* enamel bowl was perched carefully on the display stand; its beauty and fragility commanded the highest price at the auction.

VITUPERATIVE (adj) *[vahy-TOO-per-uh-tiv]*

Syn: abusive; scalding

Ant: supporting; praising; approving

Usage: She'd had enough of his *vituperative* remarks against her so she simply walked out of the room.

VOLATILE (adj) *[VOL-uh-tl]*

Syn: changeable; explosive; evaporating rapidly

Ant: stolid; impassive

Usage: His *volatile* temperament leaves them wondering what to expect each day.

(Supposition – Yeoman)

Chapter 10

WARRANTED (adj) *[wawr-uhnt d]*

Syn: justified; authorized

Ant: endangered; nullified; invalidated; repudiated

Usage: The school principal declared that the pep rally was a *warranted* use of class time, given that the school had never before succeeded through competition to the state level.

WARY (adj) *[WAIR-ee]*

Syn: very cautious; careful

Ant: unwary; unsuspecting; heedless; unguarded; foolhardy; reckless; intrepid

Usage: The villagers are very *wary* of outsiders after the bombing happened.

WELTER (n) *[WEL-ter]*

Syn: turmoil; bewildering jumble; confusion

Ant: calm; peace

Usage: The new freshmen were intimidated by the *welter* and chaos in the hallway as the upperclassmen stormed through.

WHIMSICAL (n) *[WHIM-zi-kuh l]*

Syn: capricious; fanciful

Ant: staid; serious; sober; sedate; orderly

Usage: His *whimsical*, weird nature often amuses people.

XENOPHOBIA (n) *[zen-uh-FOH-bee-uh]*

Syn: fear or hatred of foreigners

Ant: tolerance or respect for foreigners

Usage: The degree to which she practices *xenophobia* makes others see her as a strong racist.

YEOMAN (n) *[YOH-muh n]*

Syn: worker; middle-class farmer; petty officer in the navy

Usage: The *yeoman* was recognized as the hardest worker in the crew.

www.ingramcontent.com/pod-product-compliance
Lightning Source LLC
Chambersburg PA
CBHW071413300426
44114CB00016B/2286